A.K. SHAH

The Modern Side Hustler

Beyond the 9-to-5: An Ultimate Guide to Generate An Extra Income

Contents

1

Introduction

Welcome to *The Modern Side Hustler*. If you're reading this, you're likely ready to make extra money beyond your day job. You may have limited free time, but you're motivated to boost your financial security and take control of your financial future. This book is built to fit into your schedule and guide you through various side hustle options that you can dive into right away. Whether you want to earn a small income on the side or build something substantial, this guide has practical steps to get you moving.

I wrote this book because side hustles aren't just extra work—they're extra freedom. Having an additional income stream is a game-changer, but finding the right side hustle can feel overwhelming. Not all side hustles require the same time, money, or skills to get started. That's why this book is designed to help you make informed choices based on your unique goals, resources, and schedule. From simple, no-cost ideas to those that require a little investment or specific skills, this guide breaks down each type of side hustle to help you find the right fit.

In these pages, you'll find practical ideas that are easy to act on. Every chapter provides focused advice on types of side hustles tailored to different needs. First, we'll cover side hustles with no upfront costs, so you can start earning without financial risk. Then, we'll explore side hustles that capitalize on specific skills—perfect if you want to leverage your expertise. Finally, we'll look at options that involve a low-to-medium investment, so you can understand the benefits of putting in a little to earn more in return.

Each section gives you exactly what you need to make an informed decision on your own on whether any side hustle would be best for you, with strategies for taking action quickly and tips to help you maintain a work-life balance. By the end, you'll have many more ideas for creating extra income in a way that fits your life and goals.

Before we get started, as an author of this book, I would like to make a disclaimer, that the information provided in this book is intended for informational purposes only and should not be construed as professional or personal financial advice. I am not an attorney, accountant, or financial advisor, nor am I holding myself out to be, and the information that you will read in the upcoming chapters are for the sole purpose of providing you with knowledge on various ways an individual can earn an extra income. The responsibility and ownership for taking any action into any form of investments mentioned in this book lies solely with the reader and the reader alone. While every effort has been made to ensure accuracy, as an author, I encourage you, the reader, to conduct your own research and due diligence before making any investment decisions. Always consult with a qualified financial advisor to assess your individual circumstances and needs.

Here's a quote that I like to think about every time I start anything new in my life that seems hard at first:

"Believe you can and you're halfway there."

- Theodore Roosevelt -

These words, famously attributed to Theodore Roosevelt, carry a power that extends beyond mere optimism; they're a reminder of the impact that self-belief can have on our lives. Every goal starts with a spark of belief—a simple yet profound sense of "I can." Whether it's launching a new project, picking up a side hustle, or making a personal change, the journey toward anything meaningful relies on believing that our potential is greater than our doubts. Without that belief, we become our own biggest obstacles. But when we embrace it, our internal narrative changes, giving us the motivation to move forward, take risks, and overcome challenges.

Self-belief isn't just about thinking we can succeed; it's about fueling our actions with a sense of purpose. When we believe in ourselves, we stop focusing on potential setbacks or what others might think. We focus on what *we* are capable of. This confidence translates into energy that keeps us going, even when the path is tough. Challenges may come, but with self-belief, we see them as temporary hurdles rather than permanent barriers. It becomes easier to put in the work, even when progress feels slow, because we know each step is bringing us closer to our goal. We realize that success isn't about perfection or avoiding failure—it's about showing up, staying resilient, and continually moving forward.

Moreover, believing in ourselves unlocks the ability to dream bigger. Sometimes, we limit our goals based on our past experiences or the opinions of others, underestimating what we're truly capable of. But when we believe that we can do more, our goals expand. We start seeing opportunities in unexpected places, and we allow ourselves to think bigger than before. This mindset shift is essential because we're often capable of so much more than we realize. Many people achieve incredible things not because they had all the answers from the start, but because they believed they could figure things out along the way. They trusted themselves to adapt, learn, and grow.

So, take a moment to recognize that belief is more than a nice idea—it's a driving force that turns dreams into reality. By believing you can, you've already started the journey; you're halfway there. The rest will come as you keep taking steps, big or small, in the direction of your goals. And remember, self-belief isn't something you either have or don't; it's something you cultivate, one positive thought, one small victory at a time. Keep reminding yourself of what you're working toward and let that belief become your fuel. The distance to your goal is as far as you think it is. If you believe you can, you're already well on your way.

Now, let's get started. In the next chapter, we'll jump into side hustles that require no investment and no specific skills—perfect for anyone ready to dive in right now. Just remember that each side hustle will have its own advantages and disadvantages, its own challenges and benefits, its own risks and rewards. At the end of the day, you have full control of which side hustle resonates with you based on your interests, skill sets, or experience. So keep an open mind and stay curious as you read through each of the hustles that are detailed and brief.

2

Jump start Side Hustles: Earn Without Investment or Expertise

One of the best things about side hustles today is that there are so many ways to start making extra money without needing a big financial investment or specialized skills. This chapter dives into side hustle options that are accessible to anyone. Whether you've got a car, a bit of extra storage space, or just some spare time, there are straightforward ways to start earning.

Here's a look at a range of no-cost side hustles, each with its own perks. Some of these require a bit of legwork, while others can be done entirely online. The goal here is simple: to give you fast, flexible ways to start adding extra income into your life without the need to spend upfront.

Side Hustle # 1: Deliveries or Ridesharing

Deliveries and ridesharing are two of the fastest-growing options for earning extra cash without needing specialized skills or upfront investment. Both let you make money with a car, and they offer the flexibility to work around your primary job. Here's how to get started with each.

Deliveries

Delivering food, groceries, or packages can be a low-commitment way to earn side income, often with the option to set your own hours. Popular delivery platforms like DoorDash, Instacart, and Uber Eats make it easy to get started. Here's what you need to know to jump into the delivery side hustle.

Time Commitment:

- **Flexible Hours**: Delivery apps allow you to pick your shifts, and you can typically go online or offline whenever you want. Many drivers choose to work during peak hours, like lunch and dinner times, or on weekends to maximize earnings. Working during these busy times can increase your delivery volume.
- **Workload and Efficiency**: On average, a delivery driver may complete 1–2 orders per hour, depending on distance, traffic, and order wait times. Some drivers can squeeze in more deliveries per hour if they're in densely populated or high-demand areas.
- **Weekly or Monthly Hours**: If you can commit to 10–20 hours per week during peak times, you'll likely see steady earnings. You can adjust your schedule to fit around other obligations, making

this side hustle ideal if you have limited but consistent free time.

Average Earnings Potential:

- **Average Hourly Rate**: Delivery drivers typically earn between $10 to $25 per hour, including tips. Some platforms like DoorDash or Instacart may pay higher during busy periods or offer bonuses for completing a set number of orders.
- **Monthly Earnings**: If you work 10–20 hours weekly, you could make an estimated **$400–$1,200** per month, depending on your location, delivery volume, and tips. More intensive work schedules or high-demand areas could push earnings higher, but average drivers often stay within this range.
- **Additional Bonuses**: Some platforms offer sign-up bonuses, peak-time incentives, or challenges that allow you to earn more by completing a certain number of deliveries within a time frame. These bonuses can boost your income, especially when you're first starting.

Requirements to Get Started:

- Transportation: Most delivery platforms require a vehicle, but some may allow bicycles or scooters in busy urban areas. Check the platform's guidelines to see if your type of vehicle is accepted.
- Driver's License and Insurance: You'll need a valid driver's license and proof of insurance for your vehicle. Make sure your coverage meets the platform's requirements.
- Smartphone: A smartphone is essential, as you'll receive orders, directions, and customer information through the platform's app.

Step-by-Step to Get Started:

1. Choose a Platform: Start by exploring the top delivery apps—**DoorDash, Uber Eats, Grubhub, and Instacart**. Check which platforms are most active in your area, as this can impact how much work is available.

2. Sign Up and Apply: Visit the website or download the app for the platform you've chosen. You'll need to provide basic information (such as your name, phone number, and address) and upload documentation, like your driver's license and proof of insurance.

3. Complete a Background Check: Most delivery services run a background check as part of their onboarding process. This typically takes a few days, and you'll receive a notification once it's complete.

4. Familiarize Yourself with the App: Once you're approved, spend a bit of time exploring the app. Learn how to accept orders, navigate directions, and communicate with customers. This prep work can make your first deliveries smoother.

5. Plan Your Schedule: Delivery platforms often have peak times—lunch, dinner, weekends—when demand is higher. Scheduling your shifts during these times can increase your earnings.

6. Get Started: When you're ready, go online within the app to start receiving delivery requests. Accept orders that fit your route and time availability, and follow the in-app directions to pick up and drop off items.

Ridesharing

Ridesharing services like Uber and Lyft are another great way to earn money with your car. Unlike deliveries, ridesharing involves transporting passengers, which can often yield higher earnings, especially during peak times. Here's how to get started in ridesharing.

Time Commitment:

- **Flexible but Strategic Hours**: Like deliveries, ridesharing lets you set your own hours, but to maximize earnings, driving during peak times is key. These periods include weekday rush hours, Friday and Saturday nights, and special events.
- **Hourly Workload**: You may complete 1–2 rides per hour, depending on your city's demand and the distance of each trip. In urban areas with high traffic, rides are often shorter but more frequent. In suburban areas, rides may be longer but less frequent.
- **Weekly or Monthly Hours**: If you can drive around 10–15 hours per week during peak times, you'll likely find a consistent flow of rides without major time commitment.

Average Earnings Potential:

- **Average Hourly Rate**: Rideshare drivers typically earn between **$15 to $35** per hour, including tips and surge pricing. Surge pricing during high-demand periods can increase rates significantly, making peak hours more profitable.
- **Monthly Earnings**: If you work about 10–15 hours weekly, you could earn between **$600–$2,100 per month**, depending on demand in your area and how often you drive during surge pricing. If you're in a high-demand urban area, working primarily during surge hours could bring in even more.
- **Bonuses and Incentives**: Both Uber and Lyft offer bonuses, particularly for new drivers or for completing a set number of rides within a certain time frame. These bonuses can add to your monthly earnings and are often available during busy weekends and holidays.

Requirements to Get Started:

- Vehicle: Your car will need to meet certain requirements based on age, size, and condition. Uber and Lyft both have specific standards, which may vary depending on your location.
- Driver's License and Insurance: You'll need a valid driver's license and insurance that meets state and platform requirements.
- Background Check: Like delivery services, ridesharing platforms will require a background check to ensure passenger safety.
- Smartphone: A smartphone is necessary for using the app to accept rides, follow GPS directions, and communicate with passengers.

Step-by-Step to Get Started:

1. Choose Your Platform: Uber and Lyft are the two primary ridesharing platforms, and many drivers use both to maximize earnings. Research to see which one has more demand in your area, or consider signing up for both.
2. Sign Up: Begin the sign-up process by visiting Uber or Lyft's website or app. Submit your basic information, including your name, address, and vehicle details, and upload any required documents like your license and insurance.
3. Vehicle Inspection: Many cities require rideshare vehicles to pass an inspection before driving. This ensures your car is safe and meets platform standards. Check if your platform requires this and find an inspection center in your area if needed.
4. Complete Background and Safety Checks: Rideshare platforms will conduct a background check as part of their safety protocols. You'll be notified when you're cleared to start driving.
5. Get to Know the App: Take time to learn the app's features, including accepting rides, using GPS, and communicating with

passengers. Knowing how the app works will make your first rides easier and help you avoid mistakes.

6. Plan Your Hours: Ridesharing platforms have peak hours when rates can surge, like during the morning and evening commute, on weekends, or during special events. Driving during these times can increase your earnings.

7. Start Driving: Once you're approved, go online within the app to begin receiving ride requests. The app will guide you to each passenger's location and provide directions for drop-offs, making it easy to manage even if it's your first time.

Key Considerations for Both Delivery and Ridesharing

- **Expenses**: Remember that you'll need to account for gas, vehicle maintenance, and possible insurance adjustments. These costs can vary depending on how much you drive and your vehicle's fuel efficiency.

- **Taxes**: Since you're classified as an independent contractor, you'll be responsible for self-employment taxes. Setting aside part of your income for tax purposes will help avoid surprises at tax time.

- **Driver Ratings**: Both rideshare and delivery apps use customer feedback to determine driver ratings, which can impact the number of job opportunities you receive. Providing good customer service—on-time deliveries, polite interactions, and accurate orders—can help keep your ratings high.

Both delivery and ridesharing side hustles give you the freedom to choose when and where you work, making them ideal if you're looking for flexible, immediate income. With no upfront costs, this is one of the simplest ways to start earning in your spare time.

11

If you believe this is a good fit for you, then you can give this gig a shot...

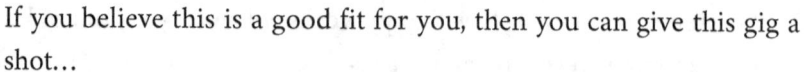

Side Hustle # 2: Rent Out Your Car

Renting out your car through a platform like Turo can provide passive income with a relatively low time commitment, especially if you aren't using your vehicle regularly. Here's what to consider about the time investment required and how much you might realistically make on a monthly basis.

Time Commitment:

Initial Setup: Setting up your car listing on Turo may take a couple of hours initially. This involves creating your account, uploading your vehicle information, setting your rates, and taking quality photos of your car. This is mostly a one-time effort.

Weekly Maintenance: Once your car is listed, you'll need to keep up with a few maintenance tasks each week. This includes:

- **Cleaning**: Keeping the car clean before each rental, which could take 15–30 minutes depending on how frequently your car is rented.
- **Availability and Scheduling**: Setting your availability in the app may take only a few minutes weekly, but keeping it consistent will help you attract regular bookings.
- **Key Exchange**: The time required for each key exchange can

vary. Some owners meet renters in person, which may take 15–20 minutes per booking, while others use remote lockbox solutions (if the platform allows) to minimize this time further.

For most owners who list their car part-time, the total time investment is often around 1–3 hours per week, with a little more time needed during the first setup and busy periods.

Average Earnings Potential:

Average Daily Earnings: On Turo, most car owners earn between $30 and $70 per day, depending on the make, model, and demand in your location. Premium vehicles and newer models tend to command higher rates, while basic models and older vehicles may earn on the lower end.

Monthly Earnings Based on Frequency:

- **Occasional Rentals (5–10 days per month):** If you rent your car for around 5–10 days a month, you could earn an estimated $150–$700 per month, depending on your vehicle's rate and local demand. This could be ideal for part-time car rentals, where you only list your vehicle on weekends or specific weekdays.
- **Frequent Rentals (15–20 days per month):** If you list your car for more frequent availability, such as weekdays and weekends, earnings can increase significantly. With 15–20 rental days per month, you might earn between $900 and $1,400 monthly.
- **Full Availability (25–30 days per month):** For those who rarely use their car and are able to rent it out nearly full-time, monthly earnings can range from $1,500 to over $2,000. High-demand urban areas and tourist destinations can drive up earnings if your

car is constantly in demand.

Additional Earnings Tips:

- **Seasonal and Location-Based Demand**: Car rentals often increase during holiday seasons, in areas near airports, or in locations with high tourist traffic. Adjusting your availability and pricing to match these peak times can boost income.
- **Extras for Added Income**: Turo lets you offer add-ons, such as GPS devices, child car seats, or prepaid fuel, which can attract renters and provide additional income. You can charge extra for these conveniences, which is an option to increase your earnings per rental.
- **Owner Protection Plans**: Turo provides different protection plans for car owners, with varying levels of insurance coverage. These plans affect your income as higher coverage plans come with a larger fee deducted from each rental. However, they can provide peace of mind in case of damage or accidents.

Here's a breakdown of what you need to get started and a step-by-step guide for launching your car rental side hustle.

Requirements to Get Started:

Car Eligibility: Most platforms like Turo have specific vehicle requirements, such as:

- The car must be 12 years old or newer (some exceptions may apply).
- Your vehicle should have fewer than 130,000 miles.
- The car should be in good condition with no major cosmetic or mechanical issues.

Vehicle Documentation: You'll need proof of insurance and registration. Turo provides additional insurance coverage during rentals, but your car must be registered and insured before listing.

Smartphone and Internet Access: Managing bookings, updating availability, and communicating with renters all happen through the platform's app or website, so reliable internet and a smartphone are essential.

Step-by-Step to Get Started:

Choose a Platform: Turo is the most widely used platform for personal car rentals. Visit Turo's website to review their requirements, insurance options, and fees to ensure they fit your needs. You may also find local car-sharing services that cater specifically to your area.

Sign Up and List Your Car:

- **Create an Account**: Sign up with your personal information and upload a valid driver's license and insurance.
- **List Your Car**: During the listing process, you'll be asked for details about your car, such as make, model, year, and mileage.
- **Set Your Pricing**: Turo allows you to set your daily rate or opt for automatic pricing that adjusts based on local demand. Research similar listings in your area to price competitively.

Take High-Quality Photos: Well-lit, clear photos that showcase your car from different angles (inside and outside) are crucial. Highlight unique features like leather seats, spacious trunk, or added amenities, as these may attract more renters.

Outline Availability: Set the days and times your car is available. You can adjust your car's availability around your schedule, making it easy to block off dates when you need your vehicle. If you have regular availability (e.g., weekdays only), try to keep this consistent for repeat rentals.

Familiarize Yourself with Insurance and Policies:

- **Turo Insurance**: Turo offers various insurance protection plans, with different levels of coverage based on what you prefer (e.g., a lower plan with higher owner responsibility or a higher plan that fully covers damages). Choose the one that best suits your comfort level.
- **Know the Policies**: Understand Turo's policies on things like mileage limits, cleaning fees, and late returns so you're prepared to manage any issues that may arise.

Prepare for Rental Days:

- **Clean and Inspect Your Car**: Make sure your car is clean and in good condition before each rental. Take a few photos to document its condition in case there are disputes after the rental period.
- **Leave a "How-To" for Renters**: Consider leaving a quick guide in the glove box that covers things like starting instructions, operating unique features, and returning guidelines.

Accept Bookings and Communicate with Renters:

- When you receive a booking, reach out to the renter to confirm pickup details and answer any questions they may have.
- You can either meet renters to hand over the keys or set up a remote key exchange if the platform offers that option.

Receive Payments and Reviews:

- After each rental, you'll receive payment directly through the platform. Check your earnings summary and ensure everything is accurate.
- Turo allows renters to leave reviews, so keep a friendly and responsive communication style to maintain a positive rating.

Renting out your car is a relatively hands-off side hustle, with the majority of time spent upfront during setup. By listing your car strategically, especially during high-demand periods, and keeping it well-maintained, you can consistently earn extra income with minimal ongoing time commitment. This can be a smart choice for anyone with an unused vehicle and limited spare time looking for a reliable source of passive income.

If you believe this is a good fit for you, then you can give this gig a shot...

Side Hustle # 3: Storage Space Rental

Renting out unused space in your home, such as a basement, garage, or spare room, can be an effective way to generate additional income with minimal effort. This side hustle appeals to those looking for affordable storage solutions while allowing you to monetize otherwise wasted space. Here's a detailed breakdown of the time commitment involved, earning potential, and actionable steps to get started.

Time Commitment:

Initial Setup (1–2 hours):

- **Assessing Available Space**: Spend about 30 minutes to an hour evaluating your property to identify suitable storage areas. Consider the size, accessibility, and condition of your available spaces (e.g., basement, garage, attic).
- **Preparing the Space**: Cleaning and organizing the area to ensure it's presentable for potential renters can take an additional hour. Make sure the space is clean, free of hazards, and can accommodate various items.

Ongoing Management (1–3 hours per month):

- **Listing Your Space**: Creating a listing on platforms like Neighbor or StoreAtMyHouse may take about 30 minutes. This includes taking photos and writing a description.
- **Responding to Inquiries**: Depending on demand, you may spend about 1 hour each month communicating with potential renters. This includes answering questions, arranging viewings, and handling bookings.
- **Regular Check-ins**: If you have ongoing rentals, you may need to check on the stored items occasionally, especially if you're renting out a garage or basement. This could take an additional 30 minutes to an hour each month.

Flexible Hours: One of the great advantages of this side hustle is its flexibility. You can work around your schedule and only allocate time when it's convenient for you.

Average Earning Potential:

Pricing Your Space:

- The average rental price for storage space can vary significantly based on location and the type of space offered. On average, homeowners can expect to charge between $50 and $300 per month, depending on the size and accessibility of the storage area.
- For example, renting out a basement or garage space may allow you to charge $150 to $300 per month, while a smaller space in a less desirable location might go for $50 to $100.

Monthly Earnings Breakdown:

- **Single Space Rental:** Renting one space could bring in between $50 and $300 monthly, depending on the size and location of the storage area.
- **Multiple Rentals:** If you have multiple areas to rent out, your earnings can multiply. For instance, if you rent out three different spaces at an average of $150 each, you could earn $450 per month.

Seasonal Demand: Keep in mind that demand for storage space can fluctuate based on the time of year. For example, demand often increases during the summer months when people are moving or uncluttering their homes.

Here are the steps to help you get started:

Assess Your Space:

Identify areas in your home that can be rented out for storage. Consider spaces like:

- **Basements**: Ideal for larger items like furniture or boxes.
- **Garages**: Perfect for seasonal items, vehicles, or equipment.
- **Spare Rooms**: Useful for smaller items that can fit in closets or corners.

Check Local Regulations:

- Research local laws and regulations regarding renting out storage space. Ensure that you comply with zoning laws and homeowners association rules, if applicable.

Prepare the Space:

- Clean and organize the area you plan to rent out. Remove any personal items and ensure it's in good condition for storing others' belongings.
- Consider adding shelves or storage bins if the space allows, making it more appealing to potential renters.

Create a Listing:

Sign up on storage rental platforms such as:

- **Neighbor**: A dedicated platform for renting storage space where you can create a detailed listing.
- **StoreAtMyHouse**: Another platform that connects people with extra storage space to those in need of storage.

Write a clear description of your space, including dimensions, accessibility, and any security features. Take high-quality photos to showcase the area.

Set Competitive Pricing:

- Research similar listings in your area to set a competitive price. Take into account the size of your space and any amenities you offer (like climate control or security).

Screen Renters:

- When you receive inquiries, ask questions to ensure you feel comfortable renting to them. Verify their identity if necessary and discuss their storage needs to find the best fit.

Establish Terms and Agreements:

- Set clear terms for the rental agreement, including payment, duration, access hours, and rules for what items can be stored. Having a written agreement helps prevent misunderstandings.

Maintain Communication:

- After renting out your space, maintain open communication with your renters. Check in periodically to ensure they are satisfied and that the space remains well-maintained.

By following these steps, you can easily start a storage space rental side hustle that fits your schedule and generates additional income. With minimal to no upfront investment and flexible time commitment, this option is a practical way to monetize unused space in your home while helping others find affordable storage solutions.

The readers must note that while most platforms for renting storage space, such as **Neighbor** and **StoreAtMyHouse**, do not have upfront costs for users looking to list their spaces, they may charge a small service fee or take a percentage of the rental income once a booking is made. For example, Neighbor typically takes a 4% cut from the monthly rental price, while StoreAtMyHouse might have similar commission structures. Always check the specific platform's terms for detailed fee information. It is still in fact a winning situation for many people, as the space that would otherwise go unused now became an alternate source of income that consistently brings in money each month.

If you believe this is a good fit for you, then you can give this gig a shot...

Side Hustle # 4: Equipment Rental

Similar to renting out a space, this is something that not a lot of people know about, but should know that they have the option to rent out equipment they own, such as cameras, tools, or recreational gear. This can be a lucrative side hustle with relatively low time commitment. This opportunity allows you to capitalize on items that might otherwise sit idle while providing others with access to necessary tools or recreational equipment. Here's a detailed overview of the time commitment involved, earning potential, and actionable steps to get started.

Time Commitment:

Initial Setup (1–2 hours):

- Inventory Assessment: Spend about 30 minutes to an hour cataloging the equipment you wish to rent out. Take note of the condition, brand, model, and any special features.
- Researching Rental Value: Dedicate another 30 minutes to researching the market value of similar items for rent. This helps you set competitive pricing. You can research your competitors on the specific platforms that will be mentioned later for the tools that you have identified to list to give you an idea of base price to work with.

Ongoing Management (1–3 hours per month):

- Creating and Managing Listings: Setting up your online listing on rental platforms can take about 1 hour. This includes taking quality photos, writing detailed descriptions, and uploading your inventory.
- Responding to Inquiries: Allocate around 30 minutes to an hour per week to respond to rental inquiries, confirm bookings, and arrange pick-up or delivery.
- Maintenance Checks: Periodically inspect the equipment for wear and tear, which may take 30 minutes each month, depending on how often your items are rented out.

Flexibility: The time commitment can vary based on how frequently your items are rented. If you have a high turnover of rentals, you may need to invest more time in communication and management.

Average Earning Potential:

Pricing Your Equipment:

The rental price for equipment can vary widely based on the type of item, brand, and local demand. You want to do some research on similar products listed on the site in your area or areas around yours to give you an idea. On average, you can expect to charge:

- Cameras: $30 to $100 per day, depending on the model and accessories.
- Power Tools: $10 to $50 per day for popular tools like drills, saws, or lawn equipment.
- Recreational Gear: $15 to $60 per day for items like bikes, kayaks, or camping gear.

Monthly Earnings Breakdown:

- **Single Item Rental**: If you rent out one camera for 10 days at $50 per day, you'd earn $500 monthly. Similarly, renting a high-demand power tool for 15 days at $25 per day could yield $375.
- **Multiple Items**: If you diversify your rentals and offer several items, your monthly earnings can increase significantly. For example, renting out three different items at an average of $40 per day for 10 days each could lead to $1,200 monthly.

Seasonal Demand: Some equipment may have higher demand during specific seasons (e.g., outdoor gear in summer), which can increase your earnings. Plan your inventory and pricing strategy accordingly.

Here are the steps to help you get started:

Assess Your Equipment:

Identify items you own that are in good condition and suitable for renting. Popular categories include:

- Photography Equipment: Cameras, lenses, tripods.
- Tools: Drills, saws, ladders, lawn equipment.
- Recreational Gear: Bicycles, kayaks, camping gear, snowboards.

Check Local Regulations:

- Research any local regulations regarding equipment rentals, such as permits or insurance requirements. Ensure compliance to avoid any legal issues.

Clean and Prepare Equipment:

- Thoroughly clean and inspect each item to ensure it's in good working condition. Consider performing minor repairs or maintenance if necessary to make your items more appealing to renters.

Create a Listing:
Sign up on rental platforms such as:

- Fat Llama: A popular platform for renting out various equipment, from tech gadgets to tools.
- PeerRenters: A marketplace for renting all kinds of gear and equipment.

Write detailed descriptions, including the specifications, condition, rental terms, and any included accessories. Use high-quality photos to showcase your equipment.

Set Competitive Pricing:

- Research similar items on your chosen platforms to determine competitive rental rates. Consider the demand in your area and the condition of your equipment when setting prices.

Establish Rental Terms:

Create clear terms for your rentals, including:

- Rental duration
- Deposit requirements (if any)
- Pick-up/drop-off arrangements
- Guidelines on care and use of equipment

Promote Your Listings:

- Share your listings on social media or local community boards to increase visibility. Word of mouth can also be a powerful tool; let friends and family know you're renting equipment.

Maintain Communication:

- After a rental is confirmed, maintain open communication with the renter regarding pick-up and drop-off details. Ensure they understand how to use the equipment properly and answer any questions they may have.

Imagine the number of tools and equipment that you own and are going unused which could otherwise be generating some extra money for you. The way I look at it is that it is actually costing you the money which otherwise would be landing into your pockets, if they were listed for use on these platforms. This doesn't mean that every single tool and equipment you have lying around would be an ideal fit for this scenario, but the chances are that most people probably will have a few that could be rented out. Best way to get started on figuring out what you could list would be to start with the analysis on the platforms to see what others are renting and use that for your idea generation.

If you believe this is a good fit for you, then you can give this gig a shot...

Side Hustle # 5: Transcription

Transcription involves converting audio or video recordings into written text. It is a flexible side hustle that can be done from home, making it an appealing option for those looking to earn extra income in their spare time. Below, you'll find an overview of the time commitment, earning potential, and actionable steps to get started in transcription.

Time Commitment:

Initial Setup (1–2 hours):

- **Researching Platforms**: Spend about 30 minutes to an hour researching transcription platforms to find the best fit for your needs. Some popular options include Rev, TranscribeMe, and Scribie.
- **Account Creation**: Setting up accounts and completing any required assessments or tests may take another 30 minutes to an hour.

Ongoing Work (5–10 hours per week):

- **Transcription Time**: The time it takes to transcribe audio can vary widely based on the clarity of the audio, the number of speakers, and your typing speed. A general rule of thumb is that it takes approximately 4 to 6 times the length of the audio to transcribe. For example, For a 1-hour audio file, it may take 4 to 6 hours to transcribe, depending on your proficiency. (**Note***: I have included pro tips for you down at the bottom to automate this process for more efficiency)
- **Editing and Proofreading**: After the initial transcription, you may need an additional 30 minutes to an hour to edit and proofread your work to ensure accuracy and clarity.
- **Flexibility**: You can choose how much time you want to dedicate to transcription each week, making it a highly flexible side hustle.

Average Earning Potential:

Pricing for Transcription Services:

- Most transcription platforms pay by the audio minute rather than by the hour of work. Typical rates can range from $0.30 to $3.00 per audio minute. For example, Rev pays about $1.00 per audio minute, while some specialized transcription services may pay higher rates for legal or medical transcription.

Monthly Earnings Breakdown:

- **Single Project Example**: If you work on a 1-hour audio file at a rate of $1.00 per audio minute, you would earn approximately $60 for that project. If you can complete five such projects in a week, your weekly earnings could reach $300.

- **Monthly Potential**: Working part-time at 10 hours per week and completing about three 1-hour files weekly could lead to earnings of around $720 to $1,200 per month, depending on your efficiency and the rates of the platform you choose.

Potential for Growth: As you gain experience and speed, you may be able to take on more projects or move into higher-paying specialized transcription niches, which can significantly increase your earnings.

Here are the steps to help you get started:

Research Transcription Platforms:

Identify transcription services that align with your skills and interests. Some popular platforms include:

- **Rev**: Good for beginners; offers various transcription jobs.
- **TranscribeMe**: Welcomes new transcribers and pays competitively.
- **Scribie**: Provides flexibility with job selection and competitive rates.

Read reviews to understand each platform's pay structure and work requirements.

Create Accounts and Complete Assessments:

- Sign up for your chosen transcription platforms. Most will require you to complete an assessment test to evaluate your transcription skills and typing speed.

Set Up Your Workspace:

- Create a comfortable workspace with a reliable computer and high-quality headphones. Software for transcription, like Express Scribe or oTranscribe, can also enhance your efficiency.

Practice Transcription:

- Before taking on paid jobs, practice transcribing audio files to improve your skills. You can find free audio samples online for practice or use resources from transcription courses.

Familiarize Yourself with Style Guides:

- Different platforms may have specific style guides for formatting transcripts. Familiarize yourself with these guidelines to ensure your work meets the standards required by each service.

Start Taking Jobs:

- Once you feel confident in your skills, start accepting jobs through the platforms. Focus on maintaining high accuracy and quality, as this will help you build a good reputation and secure repeat work.

Manage Your Time Effectively:

- Plan your work schedule to allocate specific hours for transcription tasks. Setting deadlines and managing your time effectively will help you stay organized and maximize your earnings.

Seek Feedback and Improve:

- After completing projects, seek feedback from clients or platforms to identify areas for improvement. Continuous learning will enhance your skills and potentially lead to better-paying opportunities.

This is one of the side hustles that if you enjoy listening to audios or podcasts or watching videos, then you can generate some income out of those hobbies. Even if you're like me who only enjoys listening to podcasts or watching videos for interests relevant to you and don't want to sit there for hours and listen to the topics that aren't of interest to you, then you have the ability and the option to leverage the various automated approached mentioned to do that job for you. Automated transcription tools can significantly streamline the transcription process, saving time and effort. By choosing the right tool and following best practices, you can efficiently convert audio and video content into written text. With a proper initial setup, this can definitely start generating some additional income that you are looking for.

If you believe this is a good fit for you, then you can give this gig a shot...

_____

Side Hustle # 6 : Online Surveys and Market Research

Have you ever participated in any surveys online or offline? Most people would say yes to that question. More often than not, you have probably done some type of a survey in your life at one point. Especially with the way the technology is advanced nowadays, a lot of messaging chats like Whatsapp and Microsoft Teams for corporate offers surveys or polls for users to answer. The purpose of these surveys is for data gathering. Online surveys and market research gather valuable insights about consumer preferences, behaviors, and attitudes, helping businesses and organizations develop products and optimize marketing strategies. These surveys are typically created by market research firms, corporations, nonprofits, government agencies, and tech companies to inform decisions that drive growth and improve customer experiences. This option is ideal for those looking for a flexible, low-commitment way to make money in their spare time. Below, you'll find details on time commitments, earning potential, and actionable steps to get started.

Time Commitment:

Initial Setup (1-2 hours):

- **Researching Platforms**: Spend about 30 minutes to an hour identifying reputable survey sites, reading reviews, and signing up for a few to find the ones that best suit your needs.
- **Profile Setup**: Creating profiles on these platforms may take another 30 minutes, as you'll need to provide demographic information to match you with relevant surveys.

Ongoing Participation (2-8 hours per week):

- **Survey Completion**: The time required for completing surveys can vary widely based on the length and complexity of each survey. On average, short surveys typically take 5–15 minutes to complete and longer surveys can range from 20 minutes to an hour.
- **Flexibility**: You can choose how many surveys you want to complete, making this a highly flexible side hustle. Some users spend a few hours on weekends or in their spare time after work.

Potential for Daily Participation:

- Some platforms offer daily surveys, allowing you to log in regularly and complete them whenever you have free time.

Average Earning Potential:
Compensation Structure:

- **Payment per Survey**: Most survey platforms offer compensation ranging from **$0.50 to $5.00** for short surveys; **$10.00 to $50.00** for more in-depth or specialized surveys (like product testing or focus groups).
- Some platforms reward users with points that can be redeemed for cash, gift cards, or products.

Monthly Earnings Breakdown:

- If you complete 5 short surveys each week at an average of $2.50 per survey, that totals $12.50 per week, or approximately **$50 per month**.
- If you complete 2 longer surveys (around $10 each) in addition to

short surveys, you could earn an extra **$20** per week, totaling about **$100 per month**.

- **Overall Potential**: Active participants who dedicate 5–8 hours per week and are strategic about selecting higher-paying surveys could potentially earn between **$200 to $500** monthly.

Additional Earnings:

- Some platforms offer bonuses or referral programs, providing extra income for referring friends or completing a certain number of surveys within a specific timeframe.

Here are the steps to help you get started:

Research and Sign Up for Reputable Survey Platforms:
Consider starting with a few popular and trusted survey sites, such as:

- **Swagbucks**: Earn points for surveys, shopping, and watching videos; redeem points for cash or gift cards.
- **Survey Junkie**: Focused exclusively on surveys; offers a straight-forward payout system.
- **Pinecone Research**: Invites only, but pays well for product testing and surveys.
- **Toluna**: Offers surveys and rewards for participating in polls and discussions.

Complete Your Profile:

- After signing up, fill out your profile with accurate demographic information. This helps match you with relevant surveys and increases your chances of being invited to participate in higher-paying opportunities.

Check for Surveys Regularly:

- Log in daily or several times a week to check for new surveys. Some platforms will send email notifications when new surveys are available.

Set a Schedule:

- Determine how much time you want to dedicate each week to taking surveys. Consistency is key, so try to allocate specific blocks of time to maximize your earning potential.

Prioritize Higher-Paying Surveys:

- Focus on surveys that offer better compensation for your time. Review survey lengths and payouts before committing to ensure you're making the most of your efforts.

Keep Track of Your Earnings:

- Maintain a simple log of how much you earn from each platform and the time spent on surveys. This helps you assess which platforms are the most profitable and worth your time.

Refer Friends:

- Take advantage of referral programs on survey sites to boost your earnings. Many platforms offer bonuses for each friend you refer who signs up and completes their first survey.

Participate in Focus Groups or Product Testing:

- Explore opportunities beyond standard surveys, such as focus groups or product testing, which often pay significantly more. Check platforms like Respondent or UserTesting for these options.

Think of this hustle as not only a means to meet the ends that creates additional income for you, but also a way for you to directly and/or indirectly provide valuable data points that goes into the way the companies operate and create products and the customer experience around. Your experience, knowledge or simply just your opinions could help them shape the research and development for everyday use products and services. And the bright side is you don't get to do it for free. Hence,with a bit of dedication and strategy, you can turn your opinions into cash while enjoying the flexibility of this side gig.

If you believe this is a good fit for you, then you can give this gig a shot...

Side Hustle # 7: Selling Secondhand Items

If you have someone in your house like my mother, who likes to hoard things, or you simply have things that you've used but no longer see the use of anymore, then there's a very good chance you are sitting on some inventory that can possibly generate some extra cash for you. Selling secondhand items is an accessible and rewarding side hustle that will allow you to unclutter your homes while generating extra income. This option is particularly appealing for those who want to make some money with minimal upfront investment. Below, you'll find details on the time commitment, earning potential, and actionable steps to get started.

Time Commitment:

Initial Setup (2-5 hours):

- **Decluttering and Inventory**: Spend 1-3 hours going through your belongings to identify items you no longer need or use. Consider clothing, electronics, furniture, and household items.
- **Researching Market Value**: Take 30 minutes to 1 hour to research the market value of your items. Check similar listings on various platforms to set competitive prices.

Listing Items (1-3 hours):

- **Photography**: Spend about 30 minutes to an hour taking high-quality photos of each item. Good lighting and clear images can significantly increase the likelihood of a sale.
- **Creating Listings**: Allocate 1-2 hours to write detailed descriptions and list your items on chosen platforms. Highlight key features, conditions, and any flaws.

Ongoing Management (1-4 hours per week):

- **Communication and Sales**: Respond to inquiries, negotiate prices, and manage sales. This may take a few minutes to a couple of hours each week, depending on your activity level and how many items you have listed.

- **Shipping or Delivery**: If you sell items that need to be shipped or delivered, factor in additional time for packing and transportation.

Average Earning Potential:

Earnings Breakdown:

The amount you can earn selling secondhand items largely depends on what you're selling and the condition of the items. Common items include:

- **Clothing**: $5 to $50 per item.
- **Electronics**: $20 to $300+ depending on the item's brand and condition.
- **Furniture**: $50 to $500 depending on the piece.

If you sell 10 items a month at an average of $20 each, you could make around **$200** monthly. Selling higher-value items can significantly increase your earnings.

Factors Influencing Earnings:

- The condition of items, brand recognition, and seasonal demand (like holiday decorations) can impact your earning potential.

Potential for Reselling:

- Additionally, you can source free or low-cost items (e.g., from garage sales, thrift stores, or online marketplaces) to flip for a profit, increasing your earnings further.

Here are the steps to help you get started:

Identify Items to Sell:

- Go through your home and identify items you no longer use or need. Consider clothing, electronics, books, furniture, and collectibles.

Research and Set Prices:

- Research the current market value of your items on platforms like eBay, Facebook Marketplace, or Poshmark. Use this information to set competitive prices that attract buyers.

Choose Selling Platforms:
Select the platforms that best fit your items. Popular options include:

- **eBay**: Great for a wide variety of items.
- **Facebook Marketplace**: Local selling for larger items and no shipping required.
- **Poshmark**: Focused on clothing and accessories.
- **Craigslist**: Good for larger items or local sales.

Take Quality Photos:

- Capture clear, well-lit images of each item from multiple angles. Make sure to include any flaws or unique features in your photos.

Write Compelling Descriptions:

- Create detailed listings, including brand names, sizes, conditions, and any relevant information. Be honest about the condition to build trust with potential buyers.

List Your Items:

- Post your items on chosen platforms. Ensure to use relevant tags or keywords to help users find your listings.

Communicate with Potential Buyers:

- Be responsive to inquiries and negotiations. Answer questions promptly and provide additional information if needed.

Plan for Delivery or Shipping:

- Determine how you will deliver items. For local sales, arrange meeting points that are safe and convenient. For shipping, have packing materials ready and know the shipping costs in advance.

Have you heard the saying "one man's garbage is another man's treasure"? Not necessarily just a man's, but also a woman's, but if you've heard it or not, it is completely true. Many people like to buy second-hand items for multiple different reasons. Some will buy them because they don't have the luxury to spend on new items, or they don't see the need to, some do it because they want to buy and flip them for a quick profit, and some do it because they're creative and they see a use of it that's completely outside of the box. Regardless of the reason, there are always people looking to take things off of your hand nowadays simply because the secondhand items come with a lower sticker price than going out to buy a brand new or a latest model of it. Especially with the availability of tools at your fingertips, you can very easily list and sell things that you own, which you no longer desire to use. It's also a practical way to declutter your space while generating extra income, and the flexibility allows you to work at your own pace.

If you believe this is a good fit for you, then you can give this gig a shot...

Side Hustle # 8: User Testing and Feedback

With the increasing amount of use of technology everyday by almost everyone, all of us are getting more and more familiar with how websites should work or how an app should perform. When we use different websites or apps, subconsciously or consciously our mind just figures out how that site and or app works. This gives us an advantage of having experienced through numerous sites and apps which we can now also leverage to generate an income for us. User testing and feedback is an excellent side hustle that would allow you to earn money by sharing your opinions on websites, apps, and products. This role helps companies refine their offerings, ensuring a better user experience. Below are some details for this gig that might interest you.

Time Commitment:

Initial Setup (1-2 hours):

- **Profile Creation**: Allocate about 30 minutes to create profiles on user testing platforms. Provide basic information and preferences to help match you with suitable testing opportunities.
- **Familiarization**: Spend about 30 minutes to an hour familiarizing

yourself with how user testing works, including what types of tasks you might encounter and how to provide effective feedback.

Testing Sessions (1-3 hours per week):

- **Duration of Tests**: Individual user testing sessions typically last between 10 to 30 minutes. You may have multiple sessions each week, depending on availability.
- **Flexibility**: Testing sessions can be done at your convenience, allowing you to fit them into your schedule as needed.

Feedback and Reporting (0.5-1 hour per session):

- After each session, you may need to fill out a brief survey or provide additional comments. This process usually takes around 5 to 15 minutes.

Average Earning Potential:

Earnings Breakdown:

The amount you can earn from user testing varies by platform and task complexity. Generally, you can expect:

- **Basic Tests**: $10 to $20 per test, typically lasting 10-30 minutes.
- **More Complex Tests**: $30 to $100 or more for longer sessions or in-depth feedback.

If you complete 4-5 tests a week at an average of $15 each, you could earn around $240 to $300 monthly.

Factors Influencing Earnings:

- The availability of tests, your profile's demographic fit, and the platforms you join can affect your earning potential. Some platforms may also offer bonuses or higher pay for particular tests.

<u>**Here are the steps to help you get started:**</u>

Choose User Testing Platforms:
Research and select reliable user testing platforms. Some popular options include:

- **UserTesting**: Known for website and app testing.
- **TryMyUI**: Focused on user experience testing for websites and apps.
- **Respondent**: Offers more specialized studies and pays higher rates.
- **Testbirds**: Covers a variety of digital products and offers opportunities for feedback.

Create Your Profile:

- Sign up for the platforms you choose and complete your profile. Be honest and detailed about your demographic information, interests, and experience to help match you with relevant tests.

Familiarize Yourself with Testing Guidelines:

- Each platform will provide guidelines for testing. Take time to read these instructions to understand how to perform effectively and provide valuable feedback.

Start Participating in Tests:

- Look for available tests on your chosen platforms and sign up for those that match your profile. Be proactive in checking for new tests, as availability can change frequently.

Complete Testing Sessions:

- During each test, follow the instructions provided and share your thoughts as you navigate the website or app. Speak your thoughts aloud (if required) to give testers insight into your experience.

Submit Feedback:

- After completing each session, provide additional feedback through any post-test surveys or questionnaires. Be specific about what worked well and what could be improved.

Monitor Earnings and Participation:

- Track your completed tests and earnings. Many platforms will provide a dashboard for this purpose. Regular participation can help increase your chances of receiving more testing opportunities.

Consider Specialized Tests:

- Some platforms offer higher-paying opportunities for specific demographic groups or industries. Stay updated on any available higher-paying tests and apply as needed.

Whether you're a tech-savvy person or not, if you have experience in using anything over the internet at all, then this might be a good fit for you to consider spending your spare time on to test as and when you'd like and specifically what tests you'd like to engage in based on your experience and interest. This flexible option will allow you to earn money while helping companies enhance their products and services, making your feedback valuable and appreciated.

If you believe this is a good fit for you, then you can give this gig a shot...

Side Hustle # 9: Mystery Shopping

Mystery shopping is a unique side hustle that allows individuals to evaluate customer service, store environments, and product quality while earning extra money. As a mystery shopper, you'll visit businesses undercover and provide detailed feedback on your experience, helping companies improve their services. Below are the details on time commitment, earning potential, and actionable steps to get started.

Time Commitment:

Initial Setup (1-3 hours):

- **Registration**: It typically takes about 30 minutes to 1 hour to register with mystery shopping companies. This includes providing personal information, preferences, and sometimes taking a brief training or quiz to ensure understanding of the requirements.
- **Research**: Spend an additional 30 minutes to 1 hour researching

companies to find reputable mystery shopping firms that align with your interests.

Shopping Assignments (1-3 hours each):

- **Assignment Duration**: Each mystery shopping assignment usually takes between 30 minutes to 1.5 hours, including the time spent shopping and filling out the report afterward.
- **Follow-Up Reporting**: After the shopping experience, you may need to allocate another 30 minutes to an hour to complete a detailed report on your findings.

Ongoing Commitment (Varies):

- The number of assignments you take on each week is flexible and can vary based on your availability. On average, you might complete 1-3 assignments per week.

Average Earning Potential:

Earnings Breakdown:

The amount you can earn from mystery shopping can vary widely based on the type of assignment and the company. Typically, you can expect:

- **Standard Assignments**: $10 to $25 for simple store visits.
- **Detailed Assignments**: $50 to $100 or more for more complex assignments that require additional tasks, such as purchasing a product or evaluating a service.

If you complete 2 assignments per week at an average of $20 each, you could earn around **$160 monthly**. Engaging in more detailed assignments or additional shops can boost your earnings significantly.

Compensation for Purchases:

- Some mystery shopping assignments may reimburse you for your purchases, meaning you won't have to spend money out of pocket, increasing your overall profit.

Here are the steps to help you get started:

Find Reputable Mystery Shopping Companies:
Research and select credible mystery shopping companies. Popular options include:

- **Mystery Shopping Providers Association (MSPA)**: A great resource for finding legitimate companies.
- **BestMark**: Known for its variety of assignments across different sectors.
- **IntelliShop**: Offers a range of mystery shopping opportunities and pays promptly.

Register and Create Your Profile:

- Sign up for the mystery shopping companies you choose and complete your profile. Include relevant information, such as your shopping preferences, demographics, and available times to take assignments.

Familiarize Yourself with Mystery Shopping Guidelines:

- Read through the guidelines provided by each company to understand their specific requirements. Knowing what is expected can help you succeed in your assignments.

Browse Available Assignments:

- After registering, regularly check for available assignments on the company's website. Sign up for assignments that fit your interests and availability.

Prepare for Each Assignment:

- Review the assignment details thoroughly before heading out. Understand what you need to evaluate and any specific instructions provided by the company.

Conduct the Mystery Shop:

- Go to the assigned location and act naturally as a regular customer. Pay attention to the quality of service, cleanliness, and overall experience. Take notes during or immediately after your visit to help you remember key details for your report.

Complete the Report:

- After your shopping experience, fill out the required report detailing your findings. Be as thorough and honest as possible, as this feedback is crucial for businesses.

Track Your Earnings:

- Keep track of your completed assignments and earnings. Most companies will provide a dashboard for monitoring your work. This will help you gauge your profitability and adjust your strategy as needed.

If you enjoy walking around the stores to shop or even window shop, then this would be a good opportunity for you to consider. This flexible and enjoyable option allows you to earn money while helping businesses improve their customer experience, making your contributions valuable.

If you believe this is a good fit for you, then you can give this gig a shot...

Side Hustle # 10 : Pet Sitting or Dog Walking

Are you a pet lover? Do you enjoy spending time with animals and/or pets, whether they're yours or someone else's? If so, this would be a perfect hustle for you to do what you love doing, which is spending time with the animals, while generating a side income to go along with it. It's a double win situation for someone like you! As a pet sitter or dog walker, you can choose to care for animals in their owner's homes or offer dog walking services on your own schedule. Let's take a peek into what it means for this gig in terms of the time commitment, earning potential, and how to get started.

Time Commitment:

Initial Setup (1-2 hours):

- Profile Creation: Setting up a profile on pet care platforms like Rover or Wag! will take around 30 minutes to 1 hour. This includes adding information about your experience, availability, and setting your rates.
- Background Check and Orientation: Some platforms require a brief orientation or a background check, which could take an additional hour.

Pet Sitting (Flexible):

- Pet Sitting Stays: If you're doing overnight pet sitting, expect to commit the entire night to the job, although you'll have downtime during the stay. You can still engage in other activities, but you'll need to be present for feedings, walks, and general companionship.
- Daily Visits: For drop-in visits, plan to spend 30-60 minutes per visit, typically twice a day. This option allows for more flexibility, especially if you're managing multiple clients.

Dog Walking (Variable):

- Walk Length: Dog walks can range from 20 to 60 minutes, depending on client preferences and the dog's energy level. Many walkers choose to handle multiple clients by scheduling walks back-to-back.

Ongoing Commitment (Up to 10 hours a week):

- The number of clients and time you dedicate weekly is flexible. Most pet sitters and walkers with part-time availability spend between 5 to 10 hours weekly, including commuting time.

Average Earning Potential:

Earnings Breakdown:
For both pet sitting and dog walking, earnings vary based on location, experience, and demand. Generally, you can expect:

- Dog Walking: $15 to $25 per walk, depending on the area and walk length. If you walk two dogs back-to-back daily, you could earn around $300 monthly.
- Pet Sitting: $25 to $75 per day, with overnight stays paying on the higher end. If you do three overnight stays per month, you could earn around $225 to $600 monthly.

Additional Opportunities:

- Some clients may request extra services, like administering medications or providing grooming assistance, which may boost your pay rate. You can also increase earnings by taking on multiple clients, especially for dog walking.

Here are the steps to help you get started:

Choose a Platform:

- Popular platforms like **Rover** and **Wag!** are well-regarded for connecting pet sitters and walkers with clients. You can also use local social media groups or community bulletin boards to find clients independently.

Create a Standout Profile:

- Set up your profile on your chosen platform, making sure to include details about your pet care experience, availability, and what makes you a trustworthy sitter or walker. Add a friendly profile photo, highlight any relevant experience, and specify your preferred types of pets or care.

Get Certified (Optional but Beneficial):

- Some platforms offer training or certification in pet care, which can boost your credibility and attract more clients. For example, Pet Sitters International offers a "Certified Professional Pet Sitter" program.

Set Your Rates and Availability:

- Decide on a pricing structure and update your availability to avoid scheduling conflicts. Rates vary based on your location, experience, and the level of service provided, so it's a good idea to research what local sitters and walkers are charging.

Gather Supplies and Prepare:

- Basic supplies include a sturdy leash, waste bags, treats, and water for walks. For pet sitting, you might also want items like a pet carrier (if needed) and first-aid supplies. Familiarize yourself with handling different breeds and temperaments.

Accept Assignments and Build Your Clientele:

- Once your profile is live, start accepting assignments that fit your schedule. Be consistent in showing up on time, communicating well with pet owners, and providing excellent care. Building a good reputation can lead to repeat clients and referrals.

Request Reviews from Clients:

- After each job, ask clients to leave reviews on your profile. Positive feedback will help attract more clients and build trust, increasing your chances of being hired for future assignments.

Let this opportunity help you knock down two pins with one bowl (because we're animal lovers and we don't want to hurt the birds) by allowing you to spend quality time with animals and help you earn the extra cash that you were looking for.

If you believe this is a good fit for you, then you can give this gig a shot...

In this chapter, we explored a variety of side hustles that require no upfront investment or specialized skills—ideal for anyone looking to get started quickly with minimal risk. We broke down opportunities ranging from renting out your car or storage space to managing short-term or event rentals, offering practical guidance on each. Whether you're hoping to earn a steady side income or monetize your unused assets, these options are accessible and flexible, allowing you to fit extra income generation around your existing schedule. By implementing any of these side hustles, readers can create a reliable stream of income without needing any special expertise.

While these low-barrier opportunities are excellent starting points, the next chapter will dive into side hustles that leverage specialized skills, from freelance services to skill-based consulting. These hustles often offer even higher earning potential and open doors to more personalized, rewarding work. If you're ready to bring your unique skills into your side hustle journey, keep reading.

3

Turning Talents into Income: Skill-Based Side Hustles

I n this chapter, we're diving into an exciting world of side hustles that allow you to tap into the specialized skills you've cultivated over the years. Whether you've honed your abilities through education, practice, or simply by following your passion, these opportunities let you turn your expertise into extra income. Imagine being able to work on projects that resonate with you while earning money at the same time! These aren't just any side hustles; they're avenues for you to showcase what you already excel at, making your side gig not only profitable but also personally fulfilling.

Unlike the hustle and bustle of jobs that require no skills, these side hustles can lead to higher earnings and a sense of accomplishment that comes from doing what you love. We'll explore a variety of income-generating options that align with your strengths, from freelancing and content creation to virtual assistance and online courses. Get ready to discover how you can transform your talents into a flexible income stream that fits your lifestyle, all while enjoying the work you do. So, let's jump in and unlock the potential that's waiting for you!

And here we go…

Side Hustle # 11: Flexible Freelancing

Flexible freelancing offers an excellent way for individuals to leverage their skills while maintaining a schedule that suits their lifestyle. Whether you're skilled in writing, graphic design, programming, or any other area, freelancing allows you to choose projects that align with your interests and expertise.

Time Commitment and Average Earning Potential:

The time commitment for flexible freelancing can vary significantly based on the type of work you choose and the number of projects you take on. Generally, you can expect to invest anywhere from a few hours a week to 20 or more hours, depending on your availability and the complexity of the projects. Starting with one or two small projects can help you gauge your capacity and gradually increase your workload as you become more comfortable.

Earning potential in freelancing varies widely based on your skill set and experience. For example, freelance writers can earn anywhere from $15 to $100 per hour, while graphic designers might charge between $25 and $150 per hour. As you build your portfolio and client base, you can command higher rates. Many freelancers report earning anywhere from $500 to $3,000 or more each month, depending on their dedication and the number of clients they work with.

Here are the steps to help you get started:

To kickstart your freelancing journey, follow these actionable steps:

1. **Identify Your Skills:** Determine what skills you possess that can be offered as freelance services. Think about your professional background, hobbies, and any niche expertise you may have. Here are some examples of skills that freelancers on these platforms leverage to make money : Writing and Editing, Graphic design, Web development, Social media management, video editing

2. **Create a Portfolio:** Assemble a portfolio showcasing your work. If you're new to freelancing and lack professional experience, consider creating sample projects or doing pro bono work for friends or local organizations to demonstrate your abilities.

3. **Choose Freelance Platforms:** Sign up on reputable freelance platforms like Upwork, Fiverr, or Freelancer. These platforms can connect you with clients looking for your specific skill set.

4. **Set Your Rates:** Research the going rates for freelancers in your field and set competitive pricing. Start on the lower end if you're new, but don't undervalue your skills.

5. **Create a Profile**: Develop a compelling profile on the freelance platform. Highlight your skills, experience, and any relevant projects, and use professional language to attract potential clients.

6. **Start Bidding on Projects:** Browse available projects and submit proposals to those that align with your skills. Tailor each proposal to address the client's needs and explain how you can help them.

7. **Deliver Quality Work:** Once you land a project, focus on delivering high-quality work and meeting deadlines. Good communication and professionalism can lead to repeat business and positive reviews, which are crucial for your success.

8. **Build Your Network:** As you gain experience, reach out to

previous clients for additional work or referrals. Networking can significantly boost your freelance career.

It would be good to start with writing down the specific skills that are unique to you. The best way to figure out what skills of yours you can leverage for freelancing would be to first know yourself what they are and then look for opportunities on the platforms I mentioned above around those skill sets.

If you believe this is a good fit for you, then you can give this gig a shot...

Side Hustle # 12 : Graphic Design

Let's elaborate more on this specific skill set that we talked about under the freelance section. If you have an eye for design and experience with tools like Adobe Photoshop or Canva, graphic design can be a profitable skill to monetize. Common tasks would include creating social media graphics, ebook covers, or logos for small businesses.

It is a vibrant and rewarding side hustle that allows you to express your creativity while helping businesses and individuals convey their messages visually. Whether you're designing logos, social media posts, or marketing materials, there's always a demand for talented designers.

Let's understand what this gig entails:

Time Commitment and Average Earning Potential:

The time commitment for graphic design can vary based on the complexity of the projects you take on and your availability. Generally, you can expect to invest anywhere from a few hours a week to 15-20 hours, depending on the number of projects and their scope. For instance, creating a simple social media graphic might take 1-2 hours, while a complete branding package could take several days. As you gain experience and efficiency, you'll likely find you can complete projects more quickly.

The earning potential in graphic design is also quite variable. Freelance graphic designers typically charge anywhere from $25 to $150 per hour based on their experience and the complexity of the work. For example, a logo design might command between $200 and $1,000, depending on the designer's reputation and the project's intricacy. Many graphic designers report earning between $500 and $4,000 per month, depending on their workload and client base.

Here are the steps to help you get started:

To embark on your graphic design journey, follow these actionable steps:

1. **Identify Your Design Niche**: Determine what type of graphic design you enjoy most. This could be anything from logo design, social media graphics, brochures, infographics, or web design. Specializing can help you stand out in a competitive market.
2. **Gather Your Tools**: Invest in essential graphic design tools. Adobe Creative Suite (Photoshop, Illustrator, InDesign) is the industry standard, but there are also user-friendly alternatives like Canva, Affinity Designer, and Gravit Designer, which may be more budget-friendly.

3. **Build a Portfolio**: Create a portfolio showcasing your best work. If you're new and lack professional experience, consider designing sample projects or offering your services to friends, family, or local businesses for free or at a discounted rate in exchange for permission to display your work.

4. **Choose Freelance Platforms**: Sign up for freelance platforms like Upwork, Fiverr, or 99designs. These platforms connect you with clients looking for graphic design services.

5. **Set Your Rates**: Research the going rates for graphic designers in your niche and set competitive pricing. Initially, you may want to charge lower rates to attract clients, but gradually increase your fees as you gain experience and build a solid portfolio.

6. **Create a Profile**: Develop a strong profile on your chosen freelance platform. Include a professional bio, a portfolio of your work, and clearly defined services you offer. Highlight your unique style and approach to design.

7. **Market Your Services**: Promote your services through social media, a personal website, or design communities. Engage with potential clients by sharing your work and providing insights into your design process.

8. **Start Taking Projects**: Begin bidding on projects or creating gigs on freelance platforms. Tailor your proposals to each client, addressing their specific needs and explaining how your skills can help achieve their goals.

9. **Deliver Quality Work**: Focus on delivering high-quality designs and meeting deadlines. Good communication and a professional attitude will help you build long-term relationships with clients.

10. **Request Feedback and Referrals**: After completing projects, ask clients for feedback and, if satisfied, request referrals or testimonials. Positive reviews can significantly enhance your reputation and attract new clients.

Let's put your creativity to work in this side hustle. Let your imaginative mind let loose and help businesses thrive with your articulate skills set.

If you believe this is a good fit for you, then you can give this gig a shot...

Side Hustle # 13 : Virtual Assistance

If you're good at managing tasks or organizing things amongst many other skill sets then virtual assistance is an increasingly popular side hustle that would allow you to use your organizational and administrative skills to support businesses and entrepreneurs remotely. As a virtual assistant (VA), you can take on a variety of tasks, including managing emails, scheduling appointments, handling social media accounts, and providing general administrative support.

Time Commitment and Average Earning Potential:

The time commitment for virtual assistance can vary widely depending on the specific tasks you take on and the needs of your clients. Typically, you might expect to dedicate anywhere from 5 to 20 hours per week. Many virtual assistants work on a flexible schedule, which allows you to set your hours around your existing commitments. Some clients may need part-time help, while others may require more extensive support, which can lead to more hours as you build your client base.

The earning potential for virtual assistants can also differ based on experience and the complexity of the tasks involved. Entry-level VAs may charge around $15 to $25 per hour, while more experienced assistants with specialized skills can command rates of $30 to $75 per hour or more. On average, virtual assistants can earn between $500 and $3,000 monthly, depending on their client load and hourly rates.

Here are the steps to help you get started:

To start your journey as a virtual assistant, follow these actionable steps:

1. **Identify Your Skills**: Assess your current skills and strengths. Common tasks for virtual assistants include email management, data entry, calendar management, customer service, social media management, and basic bookkeeping. Choose the areas where you feel most comfortable and competent. Sign up for platforms mentioned in section 5 below to take a look at what sort of skills others are leveraging for Virtual Assistant or look for what types of skills are the businesses or people looking for and see if any resonate with you.

2. **Determine Your Niche**: Consider specializing in a specific niche to differentiate yourself from other VAs. For example, you might focus on helping real estate agents, e-commerce businesses, or coaches. This specialization can help you target your marketing efforts effectively.

3. **Gather Your Tools**: Invest in essential tools for virtual assistance. A reliable computer, high-speed internet, and communication tools (like Zoom or Slack) are crucial. Additionally, familiarize yourself with software commonly used in virtual assistance, such as Google Workspace, Trello, Asana, or Microsoft Office Suite.

4. **Set Your Rates**: Research the market rates for virtual assistants in your niche and determine your pricing structure. You can charge hourly, by the project, or offer package deals for ongoing services.

Starting with competitive rates can help you attract clients, but adjust your rates as you gain experience.

5. **Create a Professional Profile**: Sign up on freelance platforms like Upwork, Fiverr, or Belay, or create a profile on dedicated VA websites. Craft a compelling bio that highlights your skills, experience, and services. Include testimonials or reviews if available.

6. **Network and Market Your Services**: Utilize social media, especially LinkedIn, to network with potential clients. Join online communities, forums, or Facebook groups focused on virtual assistance or entrepreneurship. Share valuable content and engage with others to build your reputation. This is not a must for beginners but it definitely helps over time for you to land bigger gigs.

7. **Build a Portfolio**: Although virtual assistants may not have traditional portfolios, you can create case studies or examples of past work experiences. If you're new, consider doing a few small projects for friends or local businesses to gain experience and showcase your capabilities.

8. **Start Bidding on Projects**: Once your profile is set up, begin searching for virtual assistant gigs on freelance platforms. Tailor your proposals to each job, emphasizing how your skills align with the client's needs.

9. **Communicate Effectively**: Maintain clear and prompt communication with your clients. Set expectations regarding deadlines and project scopes to build trust and reliability.

10. **Request Feedback and Referrals**: After completing projects, ask clients for feedback and request testimonials. Positive reviews will enhance your credibility and help you attract more clients.

People are looking for virtual assistance in a variety of categories for their businesses all the time. It may just happen that your specialized skill set might be exactly what they're looking for. Many, if not all, virtual assistance opportunities are remote and can be done from the comfort of your home.

If you believe this is a good fit for you, then you can give this gig a shot...

Side Hustle # 14 : Online Content Creation

Online content creation is a versatile side hustle that allows you to share your passions and expertise while potentially earning income through various monetization methods. Whether you choose to start a blog, YouTube channel, or podcast, this avenue can be both fulfilling and financially rewarding, especially if you enjoy creating and engaging with an audience.

Time Commitment and Average Earning Potential:

The time commitment for online content creation can vary significantly based on the platform you choose and the frequency of your content production. For instance:

- **Blogging**: Expect to spend around 5 to 10 hours a week writing, editing, and promoting posts, especially when you're starting out. As you become more efficient, this may decrease.
- **YouTube**: Creating and editing videos can require 10 to 20 hours per week, depending on the complexity of your content. This

includes filming, editing, and engaging with viewers through comments.

- **Podcasting**: The time commitment for podcasting can range from 5 to 15 hours per week, including planning, recording, editing, and promoting episodes.

In general, it's crucial to be consistent with your content production, as building an audience takes time and dedication.

The earning potential for online content creators varies widely based on your niche, audience size, and monetization strategies. Here's a rough estimate of what you could earn:

- **Blogging**: Beginner bloggers can earn around $100 to $500 per month through affiliate marketing, ads, or sponsored posts. As your blog grows, you could earn $1,000 or more monthly.
- **YouTube**: Once you meet YouTube's monetization requirements (1,000 subscribers and 4,000 watch hours), you can earn money through ads. Average earnings range from $1 to $3 per 1,000 views. Successful YouTubers can earn anywhere from $500 to $5,000 monthly or more with brand partnerships and sponsorships.
- **Podcasting**: Podcast earnings come from sponsorships, listener donations, and merchandise sales. While starting podcasters may earn around $100 to $500 monthly, established podcasters can earn several thousand dollars per month.

Here are the steps to help you get started:

To kickstart your journey in online content creation, follow these actionable steps:

1. **Choose Your Niche**: Identify a niche that aligns with your interests and expertise. Consider what topics you're passionate about and how you can provide value to your audience. Popular niches include travel, finance, health, and personal development.

2. **Select Your Platform**: Decide whether you want to start a blog, YouTube channel, or podcast. Each platform has its pros and cons, so choose one that suits your content style and audience preference. This will again rely on your specialized skill to help you determine which platform would be right for you. Think about writing for blogs, video creation and editing for YouTube, etc.

3. **Research Your Audience**: Once you've established which platform would be best for you, you need to understand who your target audience is and what content they are looking for. Engage with potential viewers or readers on social media or forums to gather insights into their needs and preferences.

4. **Set Up Your Platform: Blogging**: Choose a blogging platform (like WordPress or Wix), pick a domain name, and select a hosting service. Design your blog layout and create essential pages (About, Contact, etc.) **YouTube**: Create a YouTube account, design a channel banner, and write an engaging channel description. Invest in basic filming equipment (a good camera, microphone, and lighting) to improve production quality. **Podcasting**: Set up a podcast hosting service (like Libsyn or Podbean), design your podcast logo, and write a compelling show description. Invest in a quality microphone and recording software (like Audacity or GarageBand).

5. **Create Content**: Start producing high-quality, engaging content. Aim for consistency, whether that means posting weekly, bi-weekly, or monthly. Focus on providing value and building a connection with your audience.

6. **Promote Your Content**: Share your content across social media

platforms, and engage with your audience. Join relevant groups or forums where your target audience hangs out, and promote your work without being overly salesy.

7. **Monetize Your Content**: Once you've built a solid audience, explore monetization options such as: **Blogging**: Affiliate marketing, sponsored posts, and display ads (Google AdSense). **YouTube**: Ad revenue, sponsorships, and merchandise sales. **Podcasting**: Sponsorships, listener donations via platforms like Patreon, and selling merchandise.

8. **Engage and Adapt**: Build relationships with your audience by responding to comments and feedback. Monitor your performance using analytics tools, and adjust your content strategy based on what resonates most with your audience.

Here are some ideas to help you get started on the steps mentioned above:

Blogging Ideas

1. **How-To Guides**: Create comprehensive guides on topics you're knowledgeable about, such as "How to Start a Garden" or "How to Budget for Your First Home."

2. **Personal Stories**: Share personal anecdotes related to your niche, such as "My Journey to Financial Independence" or "What I Learned from Traveling Solo."

3. **Product Reviews**: Write detailed reviews of products you use and love, like "Best Kitchen Gadgets for Busy Professionals" or "Top 10 Productivity Apps for Entrepreneurs."

4. **Listicles**: Compile lists that offer value to your readers, such as "5 Essential Skills Every Freelancer Should Have" or "10 Healthy Meals You Can Prepare in Under 30 Minutes."

5. **Expert Interviews**: Interview experts in your field and share their insights, like "An Interview with a Successful Entrepreneur" or "Top Fitness Tips from a Personal Trainer."

YouTube Ideas

1. **Tutorial Videos**: Create video tutorials on subjects like "How to Create a Professional Resume" or "Beginner's Guide to Yoga."
2. **Vlogs**: Share your daily life or special events, such as "A Day in the Life of a Freelance Writer" or "My Weekend Trip to the Mountains."
3. **Challenges**: Participate in trending challenges or create your own, like "30-Day Minimalism Challenge" or "Cooking with Only $10 for a Week."
4. **Q&A Sessions**: Host Q&A sessions addressing common questions in your niche, such as "Ask a Graphic Designer: Your Top Questions Answered" or "Fitness FAQs: What You Need to Know."
5. **Behind-the-Scenes**: Show behind-the-scenes content of your work process, like "A Day in the Studio: Creating My Latest Artwork" or "Behind the Scenes of My YouTube Channel."

Podcasting Ideas

1. **Expert Interviews**: Invite guests from your industry to share their experiences, such as "Interviewing a Successful Entrepreneur" or "Chatting with a Nutritionist."
2. **Themed Series**: Create a series around a specific topic, like "The Basics of Personal Finance" or "The History of Technology."
3. **Storytelling Episodes**: Share personal stories or anecdotes that resonate with your audience, such as "Lessons Learned from My Biggest Mistakes" or "Inspiring Stories from Everyday People."
4. **Panel Discussions**: Host discussions with multiple guests on

trending topics, like "Future of Remote Work" or "The Impact of Social Media on Mental Health."

5. **Seasonal or Timely Content**: Create episodes that align with holidays or current events, such as "Holiday Budgeting Tips" or "Back-to-School Preparation Strategies."

There are unlimited ways to use online content creation to make money but there's only a few that matter for you. For that it's very important for you to deep dive inside yourself to understand what you truly love and/or what you are truly good at doing. Start by writing down the top 20 ideas that come to your mind in terms of what things you love in life and what things you're good at doing in life. This list has to be established in order for you to come up with ideas for this gig as it will be highly dependent on things that matter the most to you. So get that pencil out and get to writing down the list.

If you believe this is a good fit for you, then you can give this gig a shot...

Side Hustle # 15 : Task Platforms

Are you a handyman or do you love doing chores at home? Are you good at any tasks which you perform often at home and don't have to think twice about when doing it? If so, Task platforms provide a great side hustle option for people who want to make money performing one-off or recurring tasks, which can range from simple household chores to errands, small repairs, or even assembling furniture. These tasks are generally flexible, so you can choose gigs that fit into your spare time and manage the level of physical or mental effort you're comfortable with. Task platforms, like TaskRabbit and Handy, allow you to offer services in categories such as moving assistance, yard work, furniture assembly, cleaning, and more.

Time Commitment and Average Earning Potential:

The time commitment for task platform gigs can vary widely depending on the type of task and how often you choose to work. For example, a furniture assembly job might take a couple of hours, while a more involved handyman job could take half a day or longer. You can take on a single task in a week or stack multiple tasks in a day to maximize earnings. Since you set your own schedule, you control how much time you want to commit. Most people spend between 5 and 20 hours a week on these tasks, making it ideal for nights, weekends, or any open slots in your schedule.

Earnings on task platforms also depend on the type of work, your experience, and location. On TaskRabbit, for instance, general tasks like moving assistance or cleaning can bring in $15-$40 per hour, while more specialized services, like electrical work or plumbing, may go for $60 per hour or more. Someone working 10-15 hours per week on moderate-demand tasks can reasonably expect to make between $300 and $600 monthly, with higher earnings possible if you specialize or work in high-demand urban areas.

Getting Started with Task Platforms:

If you think this something right up your alley, then here are some steps that can help you get set up:

1. **Choose the Right Platform**: Sign up on reputable task platforms like **TaskRabbit** or **Handy**. Research each platform's guidelines, as some require you to undergo a background check, while others might have a more straightforward registration process.
2. **Identify Your Services**: Assess your skills and interests. Decide on a few service categories to offer based on what you're comfortable with, whether it's moving help, assembling furniture, running errands, or other handyman services.
3. **Set Up Your Profile**: Craft a professional and friendly profile. Include a photo of yourself and a brief bio detailing your relevant experience and any skills or certifications. A well-written profile builds credibility and helps attract clients.
4. **Price Your Services**: Research the going rates in your area for your chosen services and set competitive prices. Avoid pricing too low; offering fair rates that reflect your skills helps attract clients willing to pay for quality work.
5. **Prepare the Necessary Tools**: For tasks like assembling furniture or performing minor repairs, you may need basic tools. Having these on hand can save you time and help you start tasks quickly when a gig comes up.
6. **Schedule and Start Tasking**: Use the platform's scheduling tools to make yourself available when it's convenient for you. Accept gigs and maintain clear communication with clients about arrival times and the scope of work.
7. **Deliver Excellent Service and Build Reviews**: Positive reviews are crucial on task platforms. Complete each task diligently, communicate professionally, and build a strong rating. High ratings can lead to more and better-paying gigs as your reputation grows.

With this side hustle, you can easily tap into your hands-on skills or even simple organizational abilities and turn your free hours into income-generating opportunities. If you're skilled at problem-solving and enjoy a variety of hands-on tasks, this side hustle could be both rewarding and lucrative.

If you believe this is a good fit for you, then you can give this gig a shot...

Side Hustle # 16 : Digital Products

This is another hustle that relies on your creativity. Imagine there were multiple side hustles that you could take up to create multiple streams of income simply because they rely on the same skill sets. Well, this could be one of those for you, if you'd choose to. Creating and selling digital products is a side hustle that enables you to leverage your knowledge, creativity, or expertise into a profitable online product with the potential for passive income. Digital products like ebooks, online courses, and downloadable templates, all of which have the advantage of scalability; you create the product once, then sell it repeatedly without the need for physical inventory. This approach is ideal for people who enjoy teaching, designing, or sharing knowledge on specific topics.

Time Commitment and Average Earning Potential:

The initial time investment for digital products can be significant, as you need to create the product from scratch. Developing an ebook or an online course might take several weeks or even months, depending on its depth and your experience with the content. However, once the product is complete and live, the time commitment drops to maintenance and marketing—typically a few hours each week to respond to questions or update content as needed. This can make digital products an excellent option for those willing to put in upfront work for long-term, passive earnings.

Digital products can have a wide range of earning potential, depending on the product type, niche demand, and your marketing efforts. Ebooks and templates might bring in $5-$50 per sale, while online courses can range from $20 to $200 or more per enrollment. For example, if you sell a $25 ebook and make just four sales per week, that's an extra $400 a month. More established creators who build strong marketing funnels can potentially earn $1,000+ monthly.

Getting Started with Digital Products

Here's a step-by-step guide to help you create and start selling digital products:

1. **Identify Your Niche and Product Type**: Start by identifying a topic or skill you know well and that has market demand. This could be a niche topic in health, finance, productivity, or hobby-related areas. Decide whether your expertise is best suited to an ebook, online course, or a set of templates.
2. **Research the Market**: Look at similar digital products on platforms like Etsy, Gumroad, Udemy, or Teachable. Pay attention to customer reviews and popular topics to understand what buyers want and any gaps in available content.
3. **Plan and Create Your Product**: Outline your product to ensure it's structured, engaging, and valuable. For ebooks, start by organizing chapters and writing content. For courses, break down lessons and create video or written materials. Templates should be designed for ease of use and aesthetic appeal.

4. **Choose a Selling Platform**: Decide where you'll sell your product. Gumroad, Etsy, and Amazon Kindle Direct Publishing (KDP) are great options for ebooks and templates, while Teachable and Udemy work well for online courses. Each platform has different fees and reaches, so choose one that fits your target audience.

5. **Set Your Price**: Research competitors to determine a fair price. Consider your product's value and the time invested, but keep it accessible to your target audience. Adjust pricing based on feedback or market demand once you start seeing sales.

6. **Create Marketing Materials**: Build a product description, promotional images, or a short preview to attract buyers. Strong visuals and a clear description of what the buyer will gain are essential for conversions.

7. **Promote Your Product**: Use social media, a personal blog, or email marketing to promote your product. You can also use low-cost ads on Facebook, Pinterest, or Instagram to reach potential buyers. Share your product in online communities related to your niche.

8. **Collect Feedback and Improve**: Once your product starts selling, ask for feedback. Positive reviews boost credibility, and constructive feedback helps you improve future products or refine existing ones.

Here are some ideas that are beginner-friendly to get you started, but don't stop there. Remember, this is a hustle that requires creativity and if you're considering it then the chances are that you have the right creativity skills. So don't let this list stop that creativity here now. Explore this list and think beyond.

Here's a list of beginner-friendly digital product ideas to get you started. These are relatively easy to create with free or low-cost tools and focus on areas with proven demand:

Beginner-friendly digital product ideas:

Printable Planners and Templates:

- Monthly/weekly planners, budget trackers, meal planners, or daily habit trackers.
- Platforms like Canva offer ready-made templates that can be customized and sold on Etsy or Gumroad.

Guides and Mini-Ebooks:

- Short "how-to" guides on specific topics like decluttering, budgeting, or meal prepping.
- Use Google Docs or Canva to design and format a clean, readable document that can be sold as a PDF.

Social Media Templates:

- Ready-made social media post templates for platforms like Instagram, Pinterest, or LinkedIn.
- Design in Canva with preset layouts for quotes, announcements, or personal branding for small businesses and entrepreneurs.

Educational Printables for Kids:

- Activity sheets, coloring pages, or learning flashcards (letters, numbers, shapes).
- These can be designed simply and are popular with parents and teachers on platforms like Etsy.

Stock Photos or Mockup Images:

- If you have a smartphone or DSLR, take quality photos of objects, nature, or workspaces.
- These can be uploaded to stock photo sites like Shutterstock, Adobe Stock, or sold on Etsy as digital bundles.

Simple Online Courses or Video Tutorials:

- Create a short course on a specific skill you're comfortable with, like time management, using Canva, or basic photography.
- Use platforms like Teachable or Udemy to easily upload and sell the course content.

Recipe Cards or Cookbooks:

- Digital recipe books focusing on a niche, like vegan, gluten-free, or 30-minute meals.
- These can be designed in Canva and sold as a downloadable PDF.

Resume and Cover Letter Templates:

- Professionally designed templates for resumes or cover letters.
- Use Canva to create simple, visually appealing designs that job seekers can customize.

Workbooks and Worksheets:

- Self-reflection workbooks, goal-setting sheets, or personal finance trackers.
- Popular in the wellness and self-improvement niches, especially on

sites like Etsy and Gumroad.

Wall Art Printables:

- Simple typography prints or graphic art that people can print and frame at home.
- Canva or Procreate (for more advanced designs) can be used to create unique designs.

Side Hustle # 17 : Online Courses

If you have a skill that's teachable and it's something that you have a ton of experience or knowledge in where you feel you can help people learn it, then you can consider creating an online course. This is a side hustle that allows you to leverage your skills or expertise to reach a wide audience online and potentially earn passive income. This type of side hustle requires an initial time investment, as you'll need to plan, create, and upload your course content. However, once the course is live, you can continue to earn income with minimal ongoing work, aside from occasional updates and marketing.

Time Commitment and Average Earning Potential:

Expect to spend a few weeks to a few months developing a course, depending on the topic complexity and content length. For a beginner-friendly, 1-3 hour course, plan to dedicate around 20-40 hours total. This includes time to research your topic, outline the course, create presentation slides or visual aids, film or record audio, edit, and upload the content. Once the course is live, maintaining it typically only requires a few hours a month to respond to student questions, monitor reviews, and occasionally update content.

Your earning potential varies widely based on your niche, marketing efforts, and course platform. As a beginner on sites like Udemy or Skillshare, you can often earn between $100 to $500 monthly if your course is well-targeted and marketed. More experienced instructors or those on premium platforms like Teachable, where you control pricing, may earn $1,000 or more monthly if you actively promote your courses. Courses that cover in-demand topics or cater to specific, valuable skills (e.g., coding, marketing, or photography) often see the highest returns.

Getting Started: Step-by-Step Guide
Identify Your Topic

- Think about the skills, hobbies, or professional knowledge you possess. Topics like "basic coding for beginners," "introduction to digital marketing," or "photography fundamentals" are examples of popular, beginner-level ideas that can attract a broad audience.
- Check platforms like Udemy or Skillshare to see which topics are trending. This will give you an idea of what's in demand and help you refine your course idea.

Choose a Platform

- Consider Udemy or Skillshare for beginners since they have built-in audiences, or Teachable and Thinkific if you want to control your pricing and marketing.
- Compare features and fees, as some platforms take a larger percentage of revenue but bring in more students, while others offer a

higher degree of ownership and customization.

Outline Your Course

- Create a detailed outline covering the main topics, subtopics, and objectives for each lesson.
- Divide your content into short, manageable sections (typically 5-10 minutes per video) to keep students engaged. For example, a beginner photography course could include sections on camera settings, lighting, and composition.

Create Your Content

- Invest in a decent microphone and camera setup if you're recording yourself. For screen-recorded lessons, tools like Loom or OBS Studio can help.
- Use presentation software (like Canva or PowerPoint) to create slides if your course is instructional. Edit your videos using basic editing software like iMovie, DaVinci Resolve, or Adobe Premiere Pro.

Upload and Optimize

- Follow the platform's guidelines for uploading videos, course descriptions, and preview material.
- Craft a catchy title and a clear description that highlights what students will learn and the benefits they'll gain.

Market Your Course

- Share your course link on social media, LinkedIn, relevant online communities, or through your network.

- Consider offering discounts to early adopters or reaching out to bloggers or influencers in your niche to help you spread the word.
- With the right planning and initial investment of time, creating an online course can be a rewarding side hustle, allowing you to generate income and build authority in your area of expertise.

If you believe this is a good fit for you, then you can give this gig a shot...

Side Hustle # 18 : Event Photography

Do you like to take pictures of people and things as a hobby? Do you own an actual professional camera? If you believe your photography skills can be taken to the next level where people would pay you to take pictures for them, then perhaps this gig is the one for you. Event photography is a side hustle that allows you to capture memories at various gatherings, such as birthdays, family events, corporate functions, or small celebrations. With some basic photography equipment and editing skills, you can offer your services for a few hours at each event, making this a flexible way to generate income using a specialized skill. Unlike full-time photography, event photography as a side hustle can fit well into evenings and weekends, making it ideal for those balancing other commitments.

Time Commitment and Average Earning Potential:

Event photography can be highly flexible in terms of time. Each event typically requires 2-4 hours of active shooting, with another 2-5 hours of post-processing and editing. Depending on your availability, you could manage one or two events per weekend. This side hustle offers a predictable schedule, as events are typically scheduled in advance. However, be prepared for some time spent on client communications, setting up shoots, and organizing equipment.

Earnings in event photography vary depending on the event type, location, and experience level. Beginners can charge between $50-$150 per hour, while more experienced photographers may charge $200 or more per hour. For a small event, you could earn between $200 to $500 for a few hours of work, with monthly earnings ranging from $400 to $2,000 if you're handling multiple events.

Getting Started: Step-by-Step Guide

Assess Your Photography Skills and Equipment

- Evaluate your current skill level in photography, especially with capturing people and candid moments. For event photography, it's essential to feel comfortable taking quick, high-quality shots.
- Basic equipment includes a DSLR or mirrorless camera with a versatile lens, such as a 24-70mm, which works well for a variety of shots. If you don't own one, consider renting equipment to start.

Build a Portfolio

- To attract clients, you'll need a portfolio showcasing your style. Offer to shoot a few events for family or friends or volunteer at local community events to build your portfolio.
- Curate a selection of images that demonstrate different event

types and settings to highlight your range. Aim for 10-15 high-quality images that showcase candid shots, group photos, and environmental shots.

Set Up an Online Presence

- Create a website or portfolio page using platforms like Squarespace, Wix, or a social media page (Instagram or Facebook) where you can showcase your work. This will serve as a point of contact for potential clients.
- Use social media to post samples of your work, tag locations and vendors, and reach potential clients through local photography or event-focused hashtags.

Decide on Pricing

- Set competitive rates based on local averages and your experience level. Offer introductory pricing for early clients to gain experience and positive reviews.
- Consider package deals (e.g., 2-hour packages, including a set number of edited images) to simplify booking for clients. Be transparent about any additional fees, such as travel or expedited edits.

Promote Your Services Locally

- List your services on local platforms, such as Facebook Marketplace or community websites, and consider joining local business groups to network.
- Offer referral discounts to friends and family to help spread the word. Building relationships with event planners and local venues

can also help bring in clients.

Develop a Workflow for Editing and Delivery

- Set up a streamlined post-processing workflow with software like Adobe Lightroom or Capture One to quickly edit images and maintain consistency.
- Use cloud storage services or an online gallery (e.g., Pixieset or SmugMug) to deliver high-resolution files to clients. Establish a standard turnaround time and communicate this to clients.

Start as an event photographer for your family or friends and get them to share your work online and let the word-of-mouth referrals and positive reviews do the work for you for your next gigs. You can also invest time in refining your skills, building a portfolio, and effectively marketing yourself via an online blog or by creating a social media page on any of the platforms and post your work there for people to see. This can build a reliable income stream while capturing special moments for others.

If you believe this is a good fit for you, then you can give this gig a shot...

Side Hustle # 19 : Stock Photography

This side hustle goes hand-in-hand with the previous one; opening up another opportunity for you to make extra income. If you like taking pictures of anything from your day to day life to some extraordinary moments of your surroundings, nature or just about anything that you can turn into an art with your camera lens, then those beautiful, artistic pictures could help you make some money.

Time Commitment and Average Earning Potential:

Creating a side income through stock photography can be highly flexible, allowing you to work as much or as little as you want. However, the initial setup requires a time investment in understanding what sells, setting up a portfolio, and creating quality content. For beginners, expect to spend about 5–10 hours per week initially, as you develop and upload your first set of images. Over time, as you build your portfolio, you'll need less time for ongoing maintenance, focusing more on creating new images and uploading them regularly. To see significant income, a larger portfolio of a few hundred images is ideal, which may take several months.

Earnings in stock photography depend on the quality, relevance, and uniqueness of your images. On platforms like Shutterstock, Adobe Stock, and iStock, you might earn between $0.25 to $2.50 per download. Photographers with large, diverse portfolios (several hundred or even thousands of images) may earn anywhere from $50 to $500 monthly. A smaller portfolio may yield lower earnings initially, but as your image library grows, so does your passive income potential. Top contributors with highly sought-after content can make significantly more.

Here are the steps to help you get started:

1. **Select Your Niche and Subjects** - Choose photography themes that sell well on stock sites, such as lifestyle images, food, travel, technology, and seasonal concepts. You could start with topics

that interest you, but it's worth researching what's trending on various stock platforms to maximize earnings.

2. **Learn Basic Photography and Editing Skills** - Ensure your photos are high quality and visually appealing. If you're new to photography, take time to learn the basics of composition, lighting, and camera settings. Free or affordable online courses on sites like Skillshare or YouTube can be valuable resources.

3. **Get the Right Equipment** - You don't need top-of-the-line gear to start; a decent DSLR or even a high-quality smartphone camera can work, depending on the platform. A tripod and basic lighting equipment can also improve your shots, especially for indoor subjects.

4. **Create and Curate Your Portfolio** - Start by taking a series of shots in your chosen themes. Quality and variety are essential, so aim to capture a range of images that can appeal to different audiences (e.g., close-ups, wide shots, different angles).

5. **Edit and Prepare Your Photos** - Use photo editing software like Adobe Lightroom, Photoshop, or free alternatives like GIMP to enhance your images. Aim for clear, sharp, and vibrant images while keeping them realistic. Avoid heavy editing that can make the image appear overly processed.

6. **Set Up Accounts on Stock Photography Websites** - Sign up on multiple stock sites to increase your reach and potential earnings. Some popular options include Shutterstock, Adobe Stock, Alamy, and iStock. Each platform has different guidelines, so read their requirements carefully before submitting.

7. **Submit and Tag Your Photos** - Upload your photos to each site and add relevant tags and descriptions. Tags are critical for discoverability, so use descriptive keywords that accurately represent the content and themes in your photos.

8. **Stay Consistent and Expand Your Portfolio** - Consistency is

key. Upload regularly to keep your portfolio fresh and gradually increase your earning potential. Monitor which types of photos perform well and create more content aligned with those trends.

If you commit to this hustle and grow your portfolio, this has the potential to become a rewarding side hustle that leverages your creativity and skill in capturing engaging visuals.

If you believe this is a good fit for you, then you can give this gig a shot…

Side Hustle # 20 : Personal Fitness Training

If you enjoy working out and hitting the gym religiously and have a passion to live a healthy lifestyle, then you could turn that into an opportunity to train others and get paid to do it. As a personal trainer, you'll guide clients through workouts, help them set and achieve fitness goals, and encourage healthier lifestyles. Whether in-person or virtually, personal training offers flexibility, and with the right approach, you can tailor your services to fit around a full-time job or other commitments.

Time Commitment and Average Earning Potential:

The time commitment for personal training varies based on the number of clients and your availability. Typically, each session lasts between 30 to 60 minutes, with additional time spent on session prep and client follow-up. As a side hustle, you could start with just a few sessions per week, allowing you to invest 3-6 hours weekly. Online or virtual training also offers more time flexibility and the potential to reach more clients without commuting.

Earnings depend on your level of experience, location, and client base. In-person sessions typically range from $25 to $100 per hour, with higher rates in larger cities. Virtual sessions might average $20 to $75 per session, but you can often serve more clients due to time efficiency. With 4-8 sessions per week, monthly earnings can range from $400 to $1,500, with potential for growth as you build your client base.

Getting Started: Step-by-Step Guide

Assess Your Expertise and Certification Needs

- Determine your fitness niche, whether it's general fitness, weight loss, strength training, or a specialty area like yoga or HIIT.
- Certification may be required to attract clients and ensure safety. Recognized options include certifications from the American Council on Exercise (ACE), National Academy of Sports Medicine (NASM), or International Sports Sciences Association (ISSA). Completing these courses may take a few weeks or months, depending on your schedule.

Develop Your Training Approach and Style

- Decide on the format for your sessions—whether they'll be virtual, in-home, or at a local gym. Virtual training offers convenience, while in-person training allows for hands-on guidance.
- Create a training program template that you can customize for each client, including warm-ups, main exercises, and cool-down routines. Offer options for clients at different fitness levels to

accommodate a wide audience.

Set Up a Basic Portfolio or Social Media Presence

- Showcase your fitness expertise with an online presence, such as a website or a fitness-oriented Instagram page. Share helpful tips, demonstrate exercises, and show client testimonials or before-and-after progress (with permission) to attract potential clients.
- Use social media to post your services, share fitness tips, and connect with others in the fitness community to expand your visibility.

Price Your Services Competitively

- Research average rates for trainers in your area and consider offering discounted introductory sessions to attract clients. If you're new to training, a slightly lower rate can help you gain initial experience and build testimonials.
- Offer session packages (e.g., 5 or 10 sessions at a slight discount) to encourage clients to commit longer-term, which can help with income predictability.

Market Locally and Online

- Leverage word-of-mouth referrals, distribute flyers at local gyms or community centers, and join local fitness groups on social media.
- Use platforms like Thumbtack, Bark, or TaskRabbit to advertise your services to people searching for trainers. You could also register with virtual fitness platforms that connect trainers to clients worldwide, such as Trainerize or MyPTHub.

Establish a Client Communication and Progress-Tracking System

- Track client progress using apps or simple spreadsheets to keep them motivated and highlight improvements over time. Many training clients value personalized attention, so regular check-ins (even just a message or two between sessions) can help foster loyalty.
- Set a clear schedule and cancellation policy to respect your time and encourage clients to stay committed.

Personal fitness training as a side hustle allows you to make a positive impact on clients' lives while building additional income. Starting small and adjusting based on client needs and time availability can turn this hustle into a fulfilling venture that complements your personal fitness journey.

Here are some references for you to get started on your certifications if this side hustle is your calling:

American Council on Exercise (ACE)

- ACE is highly respected and offers a variety of certifications in personal training, group fitness, and more. They provide self-paced study options and exam prep resources.
- ACE Personal Trainer Certification

National Academy of Sports Medicine (NASM)

- NASM is known for its science-based training approach and offers multiple certification packages, including study materials and practical applications. NASM is widely recognized in gyms across the U.S.

- NASM Personal Trainer Certification

International Sports Sciences Association (ISSA)

- ISSA is globally recognized and offers flexible online programs, including a self-paced model, which makes it ideal for those with a busy schedule. They also include career services to help you find clients after certification.
- ISSA Personal Trainer Certification

American College of Sports Medicine (ACSM)

- ACSM offers a respected certification with a focus on exercise science, making it ideal if you're interested in the clinical or rehabilitative side of training.
- ACSM Certified Personal Trainer

National Strength and Conditioning Association (NSCA)

- The NSCA's Certified Personal Trainer (NSCA-CPT) is a good choice for those looking to work with clients of all ages and fitness levels. They emphasize practical application alongside theoretical knowledge.
- NSCA Personal Trainer Certification

If you believe this is a good fit for you, then you can give this gig a shot...

Side Hustle # 21 : Rent out your home

There are multiple ways you can go about renting out your own home or a spare room in your home if you had the means to do so. Now there are some instances in this gig that do not require specific skills but then there are some that do require some more legwork and some skills learning, hence, I'm adding this hustle under the category of skill-based side hustles. And the reason I'm leaving this one for the last under this section is because it has a high potential of generating a substantial side income.Having that addressed, let's first dive into various types of rental opportunities that you have and see which one would make sense for you and your situation, if any.

Short-Term Vacation Rentals (Airbnb, Vrbo, Booking.com)

Listing on platforms like Airbnb, Vrbo, or Booking.com allows you to rent out your house or a portion of it to short-term travelers. This option works well if you have a furnished space and live in an area with steady tourist or business travel. Let's take a look at the Airbnb example, specifically.

Time Commitment:

Initial Setup: Setting up your Airbnb listing can take several hours initially. Here's a breakdown of the activities involved:

- **Account Creation**: 30 minutes to set up your account and verify your identity.
- **Listing Your Space**: 2–3 hours to complete the property details, write a compelling description, and upload high-quality photos.
- **Researching Pricing**: 1 hour to analyze similar listings in your area and determine a competitive pricing strategy. More tips on the type of research are shared towards the end of this section for your information.

Ongoing Management: Once your listing is live, you can expect to spend about 3–5 hours per week managing your Airbnb. This includes:

- **Cleaning and Maintenance**: If you handle cleaning between guests, this may take about 1–2 hours, depending on the size of your space and the level of cleaning required. If you hire a cleaning service, costs can range from $50 to $150 per visit.
- **Guest Communication**: Responding to inquiries, confirming bookings, and answering questions can take about 1 hour weekly, though this may vary based on how frequently you get inquiries.
- **Check-In/Check-Out**: Meeting guests for check-in or facilitating a self-check-in process may take about 30 minutes to 1 hour per booking, depending on the arrangements you set up.

Seasonal Considerations: During peak seasons or local events, you may experience higher booking rates, requiring you to adjust your availability and manage more inquiries. Planning for busy periods can require additional time.

Average Monthly Earning Potential:

Pricing Your Listing:

- The average nightly rate for Airbnb listings varies widely based on location, property type, and season. In urban areas or popular tourist destinations, nightly rates can range from $75 to over $300.
- For example, if your average nightly rate is $100, and you manage to book your space for 15 nights a month, you would earn $1,500 before deducting fees.

Monthly Earnings Breakdown:

- **Occasional Hosting (5–10 nights/month)**: If you rent out your space for around 5–10 nights a month at an average of $100 per night, you could earn between $500 and $1,000 monthly.
- **Regular Hosting (15–20 nights/month)**: Hosting more frequently can significantly increase your income. Renting for 15–20 nights could generate $1,500 to $2,000 monthly, depending on the nightly rate.
- **High Demand Hosting (25–30 nights/month)**: If you list your space consistently and manage to fill it nearly every night, your earnings could range from $2,500 to over $3,000 per month, especially in high-demand areas.

Additional Revenue Streams:

- **Cleaning Fees**: Many hosts charge a cleaning fee per stay, which can add extra income. Cleaning fees typically range from $30 to $100, depending on the size and condition of the property.
- **Experiences and Add-Ons**: Consider offering additional services like guided tours, breakfast, or local experiences for an extra charge, which can further boost your earnings.

Understanding Costs:

- Keep in mind that Airbnb takes a percentage of your earnings (typically around 3% for hosts). Also, factor in costs for utilities, internet, and any ongoing maintenance, which can affect your overall profit.

Here's a breakdown of what you need to get started and a step-by-step guide for launching your Airbnb hosting journey:

Requirements to Get Started:
   Property Eligibility: You can list any space you have available:

- **Spare Room**: A guest room or a dedicated space for visitors.
- **Entire Home**: If you have a separate guest house or your home can be vacated for a period.
- **Unique Spaces**: Consider unconventional spaces like tiny homes, treehouses, or converted vans, which can attract niche travelers.

Local Regulations and Insurance: Research local laws and regulations regarding short-term rentals. Some cities require permits or have restrictions on rental duration. Additionally, make sure you have the right insurance coverage to protect yourself against potential damages or liabilities.

Cleaning Supplies and Amenities: Stock your rental with basic amenities like clean linens, towels, toiletries, and kitchen essentials (if applicable). Consider offering extras like coffee, snacks, or local guides to enhance guest experiences.

Step-by-Step to Get Started:

Create an Airbnb Account: Visit the Airbnb website or download the app and sign up for an account. You'll need to provide basic information and verify your identity.

List Your Space:

- **Property Details**: Enter the details about your property, including the type of space, number of guests it can accommodate, and its location.
- **Write a Description**: Craft an engaging description highlighting unique features and nearby attractions. Use clear, inviting language to appeal to potential guests.
- **Set Your Pricing**: Research similar listings in your area to set a competitive nightly rate. Airbnb offers pricing suggestions based on demand, but you can adjust based on your preferences.

Upload Quality Photos: Take high-quality photos of your space, capturing it from different angles. Include images of the bedroom, bathroom, living area, kitchen, and any outdoor spaces. Good lighting and cleanliness in photos will attract more guests.

Establish House Rules: Clearly outline your house rules, such as check-in/check-out times, pet policies, smoking rules, and any specific requirements you have for guests. This helps manage expectations and ensures a smoother stay.

Set Availability and Calendar: Update your availability on the Airbnb calendar. You can choose specific dates when your space is available and block off dates when it's not. Keeping your calendar up to date prevents booking conflicts.

Prepare for Guests:

- **Clean and Organize**: Ensure the space is clean and organized before each guest arrives. A well-maintained environment will lead to positive reviews and repeat bookings.
- **Personal Touches**: Consider leaving a welcome note or small welcome gift, like a local treat, to make guests feel special and appreciated.

Communicate with Guests: Promptly respond to inquiries and booking requests. Communication is key to building trust and ensuring guests have all the information they need before arriving.

Check-In Process: Decide on your check-in method. You can meet guests in person, provide a lockbox for self-check-in, or use smart locks for keyless entry. Make sure guests have clear instructions on how to access the property.

Collect Feedback: After each stay, encourage guests to leave reviews. Positive reviews will boost your listing's visibility, while constructive feedback can help you improve the guest experience.

Manage Finances: Airbnb will handle payments, but be sure to keep track of your earnings and any expenses for cleaning, maintenance, and supplies. Familiarize yourself with Airbnb's payout schedule to understand when you'll receive your earnings.

Mid-Term Rentals (Furnished Finder, SabbaticalHomes, Airbnb for 30+ days)

- Mid-term rentals cater to people needing accommodations for a month or longer, such as traveling nurses, digital nomads, academics on sabbaticals, or people relocating temporarily. Sites like **Furnished Finder** and **SabbaticalHomes** connect you with such renters, often reducing turnover and providing more consistent income.

- **Income Potential**: While typically priced lower than nightly short-term rentals, mid-term rentals can yield $1,500 to $5,000 per month, depending on the property and area.

- **Commitment**: Since mid-term renters stay longer, there's less frequent cleaning and guest communication. However, it's essential to screen tenants thoroughly and set clear expectations for longer stays.

Steps to Get Started:

1. **Choose a Platform**: Sites like Furnished Finder, Sabbatical-Homes, or Airbnb's "monthly rentals" section are ideal for mid-term stays.
2. **Prepare the Space**: Fully furnish and supply essentials like Wi-Fi, a functional workspace, and kitchen equipment for comfortable longer stays.
3. **List Your Property**: Highlight amenities and list it as a "home-away-from-home" for professionals or students.
4. **Screen Applicants**: Thoroughly vet each renter, focusing on their reason for needing a longer stay and checking references.
5. **Set Up a Lease Agreement**: Use a written agreement for added

security, covering rules and any special terms.

Long-Term Lease (Traditional Rental)

- Renting out your house on a traditional long-term lease (usually six months to a year or longer) provides the stability of a consistent, predictable income. Long-term tenants often bring their own furniture, which reduces your furnishing costs.
- **Income Potential**: The monthly income is lower than short-term options, but long-term rentals are more stable. Rent could range from $1,000 to $4,000 monthly, depending on location, size, and market demand.
- **Commitment**: Long-term leases require minimal involvement once the tenant moves in, making it a hands-off approach. You'll need to handle occasional maintenance, so having a property management company can be helpful if you're managing multiple properties.

Steps to Get Started:

1. **Prepare the Property**: Ensure all major appliances and fixtures are in working condition.
2. **Choose a Listing Platform**: Sites like Zillow, Realtor.com, or Craigslist can help you reach prospective tenants.
3. **Screen Tenants**: Perform background checks and verify income to ensure tenant reliability.
4. **Create a Lease Agreement**: Outline rental terms, payment schedule, and responsibilities for maintenance.
5. **Set Up Rent Collection**: Use an online system like Zelle, Venmo, or rental software to streamline monthly payments.

Event or Production Rental (Peerspace, Giggster)

- If you have a unique or scenic home, you can rent it out for events, photoshoots, film productions, or even corporate meetings. Sites like **Peerspace** and **Giggster** allow you to rent your space by the hour or day to creative professionals and businesses.
- **Income Potential**: Event and production rentals can bring in $100 to $500 per hour, depending on location, home features, and the type of event.
- **Commitment**: This is a high-maintenance option due to frequent guest turnovers and the specific setup or cleanup required. Events can lead to more wear and tear, so consider higher security deposits.

Steps to Get Started:

1. **Assess the Space**: Think about what makes your home unique—backyard, large windows, or distinct decor—and optimize for photoshoots or events.
2. **List on Platforms**: Use Peerspace or Giggster, and provide high-quality images highlighting your space's unique features.
3. **Set Rates and Rules**: Define hourly pricing, deposits, cleaning fees, and specific rules for event types.
4. **Prepare for Hosting**: Clean and organize the space before each event and establish access points and check-in procedures.
5. Post-Event Inspection: After each event, inspect for damage, address any cleaning needs, and prepare the space for future bookings.

Co-Living or Shared Housing (Roommate Rental)

- Renting out individual rooms or a portion of your home to housemates can create a steady income without needing full-time tenant turnover. This approach is especially effective in urban areas or near universities.
- **Income Potential**: Renting a room could bring in $400 to $1,500 per month per room, depending on location and amenities.
- **Commitment**: With shared housing, you'll need to balance privacy with communal living. Clear communication about shared spaces, such as kitchens or bathrooms, is essential.

Steps to Get Started:

1. **List on Roommate Platforms**: Post on Roomster, SpareRoom, or Craigslist, and clearly describe room features and house rules.
2. **Prepare the Space**: Set up basic furnishings in shared areas and ensure amenities like Wi-Fi and kitchen appliances are accessible.
3. **Screen Housemates**: Carefully review applications and conduct interviews to find compatible housemates.
4. **Create a House Agreement**: Outline expectations for shared spaces, guest policies, and shared responsibilities.
5. **Maintain Communication**: Regularly check in with housemates to ensure everyone is comfortable and address any issues.

This is an opportunity that can potentially become a passive income source for you once you have it established. If you have an extra room, an extra house, an extra condo, etc. that you are not using, you can consider leveraging it for extra income generation.

BONUS:* Tips on pricing research for airbnb:

Initial Research (30 minutes):

Identify Comparable Listings: Look for listings similar to yours in terms of size, type, location, and amenities. Spend time browsing through platforms like Airbnb itself, as well as other short-term rental websites.

Filter Search Results: Use filters on Airbnb to narrow down results. For example, you can filter by:

- Location (your neighborhood or city)
- Property type (entire home, shared room, etc.)
- Guest capacity (matching your listing)
- Amenities offered (Wi-Fi, kitchen, parking, etc.)

Analyzing Pricing (30 minutes):

- **Daily Rates:** Once you have a shortlist of comparable listings, take note of their nightly rates. Write down the average rates for different days of the week, as pricing may fluctuate between weekends and weekdays.
- **Seasonal Variations:** Check how prices change with the seasons. Look for local events, holidays, or festivals that might affect demand and pricing. Consider tools like Google Trends to see interest in your area over time.
- **Additional Fees:** Note any cleaning fees or additional charges that other hosts include in their listings, as this can impact guest expectations and your overall pricing strategy.

Specific Resources for Pricing Research

Airbnb Itself:

- **Market Insights**: Use Airbnb's built-in pricing tools, such as Smart Pricing, which automatically adjusts your rates based on market demand. This can be a good starting point for understanding your potential earnings.
- **Local Insights**: Airbnb often provides local insights that highlight occupancy rates and average nightly rates in your area, which can inform your pricing strategy.

Competitor Listings:

- **AirDNA**: This paid service provides comprehensive analytics and market data for Airbnb listings. It offers insights into average daily rates, occupancy rates, and revenue potential based on property type and location.
- **Mashvisor**: Similar to AirDNA, Mashvisor helps investors analyze potential rental properties by providing data on occupancy rates and rental income projections in specific neighborhoods.

Local Vacation Rental Groups:

- **Facebook Groups**: Join local Facebook groups dedicated to Airbnb hosts or vacation rentals. Members often share their pricing strategies and experiences, which can be invaluable.
- **Meetup Events**: Look for local meetups or networking events for hosts. Engaging with other hosts in person can yield insights into pricing strategies and local market trends.

Price Comparison Websites:

- **Kayak or Expedia**: While primarily used for hotel bookings, these websites can give you a sense of pricing trends in your area, especially during peak tourist seasons.
- **Booking.com**: This site also lists vacation rentals and can provide a benchmark for pricing against hotels and other accommodations in your region.

Tools and Apps:

- **Beyond Pricing**: This dynamic pricing tool automatically adjusts your Airbnb rates based on market data, seasonality, and local events. It provides insights into how to price your listing competitively.
- **PriceLabs**: Similar to Beyond Pricing, this tool analyzes local market conditions and helps you set a pricing strategy that reflects demand, competition, and seasonality.

If you believe this is a good fit for you, then you can give this gig a shot…

4

Building Wealth on a Budget: Side Hustles with Low to Medium Investment

Congratulations on reaching this chapter! You've already taken significant strides toward understanding how to generate additional income through various side hustles. It takes dedication and ambition to explore new avenues for financial growth, and you should feel proud of your commitment to enhancing your earning potential. As you dive deeper into this next section, remember that the investments you make—whether in terms of time, money, or effort—can yield substantial returns, setting you on a path toward greater financial freedom.

In this chapter, we'll explore a range of side hustles that require low to medium capital investment but hold the promise of generating significant income. Whether you're considering flipping thrift store finds or diving into real estate crowdfunding, these opportunities are designed for you to capitalize on your resources and make your money work for you. The potential for growth is within your reach, so let's uncover these exciting options and empower you to take the next step toward a more prosperous future.

Side Hustle # 22 : Thrift Flipping

If you like the idea of selling and/or flipping things for a profit, then thrift flipping can be a potential option for you. It's amazing how many people sleep on this concept to generate a side income. Maybe it's the amount of time and effort required of them that holds people back, but not the readers of this book. If you are reading this book, then it clearly states you are a person who takes action. And here you are. So let's get into the nuances for this gig.

Time Commitment and Average Earning Potential

Thrift flipping requires a variable time commitment depending on how much effort you want to invest. Initially, you might spend a few hours each week sourcing items from thrift stores, garage sales, or online marketplaces. Once you acquire the items, you will need additional time for cleaning, photographing, and listing them on platforms like eBay or Poshmark. On average, you might spend around 5 to 10 hours a week on this side hustle, especially when you are starting. As you become more efficient, this time could decrease.

The earning potential for thrift flipping can be significant, with some individuals making anywhere from $100 to $1,000 or more per month, depending on the items they source and their resale strategies. High-demand items such as designer clothing, vintage goods, or electronics can yield higher profits. The key is to research and find items that can be resold at a markup, so some initial testing will help you gauge what works best in your local market or online.

Here are the steps to help you get started:

1. **Identify Your Niche:** Consider what types of items you enjoy and are knowledgeable about. Popular categories include clothing, shoes, home decor, electronics, and collectibles.
2. **Research Market Trends:** Use eBay or Poshmark to browse similar items and see their selling prices. Pay attention to what sells quickly and for a good profit margin. Tools like eBay's "sold listings" feature can give you insight into past sales.
3. **Source Items:** Visit local thrift stores, garage sales, estate sales, and online marketplaces like Facebook Marketplace or Craigslist. Look for items in good condition that you can purchase at a low cost.
4. **Evaluate and Clean Your Finds:** Once you acquire items, evaluate their condition and clean them if necessary. Make repairs if feasible, as this can increase their value.
5. **Take Quality Photos:** Good photography is crucial for online sales. Use natural lighting and clear backgrounds to showcase your items. Capture multiple angles and include close-ups of any unique features or flaws.
6. **Create Compelling Listings:** Write detailed descriptions that highlight the item's features, dimensions, brand, and any imperfections. Use keywords that buyers might search for to increase visibility.
7. **Set Competitive Prices:** Price your items competitively based on your research. Consider offering free shipping to attract buyers, as this can be a significant incentive.
8. **Promote Your Listings:** Share your listings on social media or relevant online groups to drive traffic. Poshmark, for example, has a community aspect where sharing items can lead to more sales.
9. **Handle Shipping Efficiently:** Invest in shipping supplies and

familiarize yourself with the shipping process on your chosen platform. Make sure to package items securely to avoid damage during transit.

10. **Monitor and Adjust Your Strategy:** Keep track of what items sell well and adjust your sourcing and pricing strategies accordingly. Learn from your experiences and optimize your approach to maximize your profits.

Look for thrift stores in your local area or in the surrounding towns and my bet is you will easily find at least one. You can also keep an eye on some yard sales or garage sales signs as you're going about your day to day life, because those can really open up opportunities for you to find some profitable things to flip.

If you believe this is a good fit for you, then you can give this gig a shot...

Side Hustle # 23 : Amazon FBA

This is one of my favorite types of side hustle because it simply has the potential to become a large-scale business if done in the right way, but anyone can start with a small investment of a couple of thousands of dollars, unlike a traditional business which would require a couple of hundreds of thousands of dollars. Amazon FBA (Fulfillment by Amazon) allows sellers to leverage Amazon's massive infrastructure for selling products online.

With Amazon growing year-over-year, thanks to more than 50% of third-party sellers who started off small, the potential to generate a substantial income is phenomenal. You can source or create products, send them to Amazon's fulfillment centers, and they handle storage, packing, and shipping directly to customers. This model takes a lot of logistical work off your plate, enabling you to focus on sourcing products and growing your business.

With a vast audience already shopping on Amazon, using FBA can help you reach customers without needing to manage a standalone e-commerce store. It is recommended if the seller starts with an initial investment of $2,000-$10,000 depending on the model chosen, but it is highly recommended that sellers seek out online programs that teach the in and outs of selling on Amazon because that will substantially reduce the learning curve and the cost of those programs could very easily be covered in the amount mentioned above plus a ton of room for inventory and software(s) needed to do the research, etc.

Time Commitment and Average Earning Potential:

The time commitment for Amazon FBA can vary based on the scale of your business and how much effort you want to invest. It also depends on the type of model you start when selling on Amazon. For Amazon FBA, there are the following models that you can choose : Private label, Wholesale, Online Arbitrage, and Retail Arbitrage. Each model has a different level of time it takes to set up, to source, and to keep it sustained and continuously operating. However, this is definitely something you can start out small in your spare time and spend 15-20 hours initially to get the ball rolling until you have your first sale. One thing, however, the reader should note that like any other business the more time a person provides the more the business will operate on.

The earning potential with Amazon FBA can be substantial, with many sellers making anywhere from $500 to several thousand dollars per month in profit. Factors such as the type of products you sell, your pricing strategy, and your ability to market effectively will influence your earnings. Successful FBA sellers often identify in-demand products with healthy profit margins, achieving anywhere from 15% to 30% returns on their investments.

Getting Started:

1. **Research and Choose Your Products:** Use tools like Jungle Scout or Helium 10 to analyze potential products. Look for items that have consistent demand, good sales volume, and manageable competition. Consider sourcing products that fit within your interests or expertise for a better understanding of the market.

2. **Create an Amazon Seller Account:** Sign up for an Amazon Seller Central account. You can choose between an Individual account (no monthly fee but higher selling fees) or a Professional account (monthly fee but lower fees per item). Choose based on your anticipated sales volume.

3. **Source Your Products:** Identify suppliers through online marketplaces like Alibaba, local wholesalers, or even manufacturers. If you're creating products, plan your production process. Negotiate prices to ensure you maintain a healthy profit margin.

4. **Set Up Your Product Listings:** Create compelling product listings that include high-quality images, informative descriptions, and relevant keywords. Pay attention to Amazon's guidelines for optimal visibility.

5. **Ship Your Products to Amazon:** Once you have your inventory, ship your products to Amazon's fulfillment centers. Follow their shipping guidelines carefully to avoid delays or issues.

6. **Launch and Market Your Products:** Once your products are live, promote them through Amazon's advertising tools like Sponsored Products or Amazon PPC (Pay-Per-Click). You can also leverage social media or your personal network to drive traffic.

7. **Monitor Performance:** Keep track of your sales, inventory levels, and customer feedback. Use this information to refine your product selection, improve listings, and adjust your marketing strategies.

8. **Manage Customer Service:** While Amazon handles shipping, you're still responsible for customer inquiries and feedback. Make sure to respond promptly to maintain a positive seller rating.

9. **Scale Your Business:** As you gain experience, consider expanding your product line or exploring different niches. Automate aspects of your business where possible, such as using inventory management software or outsourcing customer service.

Let's dig deeper into the various types of FBA models to help you understand the differences.

Model 1: Private Label

The private label model on Amazon FBA allows sellers to create their own branded products by sourcing generic items from manufacturers, often overseas from sites such as Alibaba, and then labeling them with their unique brand name and packaging. This approach enables sellers to differentiate their products from competitors while leveraging Amazon's vast fulfillment network for storage, shipping, and customer service. Essentially, you would identify a trending product, negotiate with a manufacturer to produce it under your brand, and then list it on Amazon, allowing you to capture sales while building your brand identity. The private label model can yield higher profit margins compared to reselling existing products, as you have more control over pricing, branding, and marketing.

Model 2 : Online Arbitrage

Online arbitrage is a retail strategy used in Amazon FBA where sellers purchase products at a lower price from online retailers or marketplaces and then resell them on Amazon for a profit. This method involves identifying products that are being sold at a discount on sites like Walmart, Target, or clearance sections of e-commerce stores and then listing them on Amazon at a higher price. The key to success in online arbitrage lies in effective product research and pricing analysis to ensure that the items bought can generate a sufficient profit margin after accounting for Amazon fees and shipping costs. Sellers often use tools and software to help streamline the process of finding profitable items, making online arbitrage a popular choice for those looking to generate income with relatively low upfront investment and minimal risk.

Model 3 : Retail Arbitrage

Retail arbitrage is a popular resale strategy within Amazon FBA that involves purchasing products from physical retail stores—such as Walmart, Target, or local clearance sales—at discounted prices and then reselling them on Amazon for a profit. Sellers scout for clearance items, overstock products, or special promotions in stores, often using mobile apps to check Amazon pricing and sales rank in real-time to ensure they're making informed purchasing decisions. The appeal of retail arbitrage lies in the ability to acquire products with minimal upfront investment, as many items can be bought for a few dollars and sold for significantly more. Successful retail arbitrage relies on thorough market research, understanding Amazon's fees, and strategically managing inventory to maximize profit margins. This hands-on approach allows sellers to tap into their local retail landscape, finding unique opportunities to turn everyday shopping trips into profitable side hustles.

Model 4: Wholesale

The wholesale model in Amazon FBA involves purchasing products in bulk directly from manufacturers or distributors at a discounted price and then reselling them on Amazon at a markup. This approach allows sellers to access established brands and products with proven demand, reducing the uncertainty often associated with launching new items. To succeed in wholesale, sellers must build relationships with suppliers to negotiate pricing, secure inventory, and understand the terms of purchase. Unlike private labeling, where sellers create their own brand, wholesale sellers typically list existing brand-name products on Amazon. This model requires an initial investment for bulk purchases, but it can lead to significant profits if managed correctly, as sellers benefit from the brand recognition and customer trust that comes with established products. Additionally, wholesale allows for scalability, as sellers can expand their product offerings by continuously sourcing new items from their suppliers.

In conclusion, online arbitrage and retail arbitrage models offer low upfront investment cost and low risk opportunities for beginner sellers while private label and wholesale demands a much higher investment cost and higher risk for beginner sellers but great opportunities for seasoned sellers. Regardless, each model offers the readers multiple ways to generate income from one single platform that they can take advantage of based on their risk tolerance and skill sets. The Amazon FBA model overall can be considered as a great opportunity for someone to start a small business and eventually grow to a bigger scale by leveraging single to multiple FBA models at a time.

Side Hustle # 24 : Print-on-Demand (POD)

Print-on-demand (POD) is a business model that allows you to sell custom-designed products like T-shirts, mugs, posters, and more, without needing to keep inventory. POD platforms such as Redbubble, Printful, and Teespring handle the entire production process—from printing to shipping—once an order is placed. This model is appealing because it requires minimal upfront investment. You only need to focus on creating unique designs, while the platform handles fulfillment. POD is ideal for individuals with design skills or those willing to explore basic design creation.

Time Commitment and Earnings Potential:

The time commitment for a POD business can vary depending on the number and complexity of the designs you create. Initially, you'll need to spend time on research to understand current trends, design your products, and upload them to your chosen platform. Once your designs are live, POD requires less maintenance, although you'll want to periodically add new products or refresh designs.

On average, many POD sellers make between $100 and $500 per month if they consistently upload popular designs and market their store. With dedication and effective promotion, some sellers see higher earnings, potentially turning it into a primary income source.

Here are the steps to help you get started:

1. **Research Your Niche and Trends:** Browse POD platforms like Redbubble and Etsy to get a sense of what's selling well. Look at current design trends, popular quotes, or styles to decide on a niche, such as travel, pets, or motivational quotes. See below on some ways to help you start looking for your first product idea.

2. **Choose Your Platform:** Select one or more platforms that align with your goals. Redbubble and Teespring are popular for artists and illustrators, while Printful integrates with Etsy and Shopify if you prefer a more customizable store.

3. **Create Your Designs:** Use design tools like Canva or Adobe Illustrator. For beginners, Canva offers free, easy-to-use templates, while Illustrator gives more customization options. Focus on simple, eye-catching designs or phrases that resonate with your chosen niche.

4. **Set Up and List Your Products:** Sign up on your chosen platform and create your product listings. Upload your designs, choose product types, and add descriptions. Make sure to use relevant keywords to improve search visibility.

5. **Promote Your Store:** Market your store on social media, especially on platforms where visual content thrives, like Instagram or Pinterest. You can also consider joining niche-specific Facebook groups or using paid advertising as you grow.

6. **Bonus*: Here are several detailed strategies for finding popular themes and styles:**

7. **Use POD Marketplaces for Inspiration:**

8. **Redbubble, Etsy, and Teespring:** These platforms have trending and best-selling categories where you can observe popular designs. Pay attention to high-ranking designs in niches you're interested in, such as nature, travel, or pop culture. Note patterns in color

schemes, graphic styles, and specific themes that recur.

9. **Amazon and eBay**: Browse categories like "T-shirts," "Home Décor," or "Gifts" and check the best-seller lists. Amazon, especially, can show you trending topics people are willing to buy.

Leverage Social Media Trends:

- **Instagram and Pinterest**: Explore hashtags like #trendingtees, #PODdesign, or niche tags like #petlover or #coffeeaddict. Pinterest is particularly useful for seeing which design ideas are being saved and shared, as this can indicate potential demand.
- **TikTok**: The platform's "For You" page often highlights trending themes or quotes. Search with relevant hashtags, such as #customtees or #giftideas, to see emerging ideas.

Explore Google Trends and Keyword Research:

- **Google Trends**: Type in topics like "funny T-shirts," "graphic mugs," or "motivational posters" to see search trends. You can also refine by region, which is useful for identifying trends that might be more popular in specific areas.
- **Keyword Research Tools**: Tools like Ahrefs or Ubersuggest can reveal popular search terms related to POD products. For instance, entering "pet T-shirt" might lead you to popular terms like "cat lover shirts" or "dog mom mugs."

Analyze Competitor Stores:

- Look at successful POD stores and analyze their design themes and pricing. Observe what sells well, read product reviews to understand customer preferences, and note any niches that are underserved, where your designs could stand out.

Monitor Seasonal Trends and Events:

- Each season and holiday brings demand for themed designs. For example, holidays like Halloween or Christmas are great times for creating themed apparel and gifts, and seasons like summer may see a rise in outdoor or travel-related designs. Check the calendar for upcoming holidays or events and plan designs accordingly.

If you're looking for a low investment gig to start out with then starting a POD business is great to look into. It requires creativity and consistency in uploading and promoting designs. With time and effort, this side hustle can generate a steady stream of income, offering both flexibility and scalability for long-term success.

If you believe this is a good fit for you, then you can give this gig a shot...

Side Hustle # 25 : Real Estate Crowdfunding

If you always thought about getting into real estate, but never took that first step due to the high risk or high capital involved or you just didn't want the hassle of managing a property and tenant that is required in a typical real estate investment, then look no further. Real Estate Crowdfunding offers a unique opportunity for people to invest in real estate without directly purchasing or managing property. Instead, crowdfunding platforms pool funds from multiple investors to finance real estate projects. This approach makes real estate investment accessible to those who may not have substantial capital but want to diversify their portfolio with property-based assets. Crowdfunding platforms like Fundrise, CrowdStreet, and RealtyMogul offer opportunities to invest in residential or commercial properties with relatively low initial investment requirements.

Time Commitment and Average Earnings Potential:

Real estate crowdfunding is a highly passive side hustle. Most of the time commitment happens upfront during the research phase, where you compare platforms, read about property listings, and decide on your investment preferences. Once you've made your investment, it requires minimal time to maintain. Occasionally, investors might check the platform for updates or quarterly reports on their projects, but this takes only a few minutes per month.

Earnings vary based on the platform, the property's location, and the type of real estate investment. Most crowdfunding investments in real estate yield returns through rental income and property appreciation, which means that the potential earnings could range from 6% to 12% annually. This could result in anywhere from a few hundred to several thousand dollars per year, depending on your investment amount and the project's success. However, real estate crowdfunding is typically a long-term investment, with earnings accumulating over time rather than providing quick payouts.

Getting Started in Real Estate Crowdfunding: Step-by-Step

1. **Determine Your Budget**: Decide on the amount you are comfortable investing. Crowdfunding platforms usually have minimum

investment requirements, which can range from as low as $10 to $500 or more, depending on the platform and the project.

2. **Research Platforms**: Look into reputable platforms like Fundrise, CrowdStreet, or RealtyMogul. Each has different property options, minimum investment amounts, and risk levels.Review user feedback and check for fees, redemption options, and any required holding periods.

3. **Create an Account and Complete Verification**: Sign up on your chosen platform, create your profile, and verify your identity as required. This often includes uploading identification and completing a brief suitability questionnaire to assess investment goals and risk tolerance.

4. **Browse Investment Opportunities**: Explore the property listings on the platform and select projects that match your financial goals and risk comfort. Some platforms offer diversified funds, while others provide individual property options for customization.

5. **Make Your Investment**: Once you've selected a project or fund, commit the necessary funds. Afterward, your money will be pooled with other investors to finance the project.

6. **Monitor Your Investment**: Periodically check for updates on project performance and any distributions. Most platforms offer quarterly or annual reports, giving insights into rental income, property appreciation, and any changes in the project's status.

Real estate crowdfunding can be a solid way to dip into property investments while keeping other commitments light, making it ideal for those looking to grow passive income without active involvement.

Below you will see a detailed breakdown of three platforms mentioned earlier to help you make the best choice based on your investment goals, budget, and risk tolerance.

Fundrise

- **Target Audience**: Fundrise is ideal for beginners or investors looking to start with lower minimums and build a diversified portfolio over time.
- **Minimum Investment**: Fundrise has a low minimum investment of $10, making it accessible to most investors. They offer different account levels, starting with the "Starter Portfolio," which gradually expands to higher-tier accounts with higher minimums and benefits.
- **Investment Options**: Fundrise offers diversified funds called "eREITs" (real estate investment trusts) and "eFunds," which invest in both residential and commercial properties across the U.S. Investors can choose between core plans such as "Starter," "Core," "Advanced," and "Premium," each catering to different investment levels and offering various asset mixes.
- **Expected Returns**: Fundrise reports average annual returns between 8-12%, though actual results can vary based on market conditions.
- **Liquidity**: Fundrise investments have limited liquidity, with holding periods typically ranging from 5-7 years. The platform does offer a redemption option, though early withdrawal fees may apply.
- **Fees**: Fundrise charges an annual asset management fee of around 1%, which covers fund management and administrative costs.

CrowdStreet

- **Target Audience**: CrowdStreet caters to accredited investors, meaning individuals with a net worth of over $1 million or an income exceeding $200,000 annually (or $300,000 with a spouse). It's geared toward experienced investors interested in more personalized, high-stakes investments.

- **Minimum Investment**: CrowdStreet generally has higher minimums, typically starting at $25,000 per investment, making it a better fit for individuals who are comfortable with a larger commitment.

- **Investment Options**: CrowdStreet offers individual deals, diversified funds, and tailored portfolios. It focuses mainly on commercial real estate projects, including office buildings, multifamily residences, and industrial properties across the U.S. Investors can view each project's details and select individual properties based on their preferences.

- **Expected Returns**: Returns vary widely depending on the specific project but can range from 7-18%, depending on the asset class and deal structure.

- **Liquidity**: CrowdStreet is designed for long-term investments, often with holding periods of 5-10 years. Due to the nature of individual commercial projects, there's very limited liquidity, and investors must be prepared to keep funds tied up until the project's term concludes.

- **Fees**: Fees depend on the specific project or fund but typically include a 0.50% to 2.5% management fee along with possible additional sponsor fees per project.

RealtyMogul

- **Target Audience**: RealtyMogul is suitable for both accredited and non-accredited investors, with a range of options catering to different investment levels and experience.

- **Minimum Investment**: The minimum investment varies; non-accredited investors can start with as little as $5,000 for REITs, while accredited investors may have minimums of $25,000 or more for individual projects.

- **Investment Options**: RealtyMogul offers two public non-traded REITs: Income REIT (focused on cash flow-producing properties) and Apartment Growth REIT (aimed at properties with potential for appreciation). Additionally, accredited investors can access private placements in specific real estate projects, which are vetted and managed by third-party sponsors.

- **Expected Returns**: REITs tend to yield annual returns around 6-8% based on cash flow, while individual projects might offer higher returns, depending on the specific deal's performance.

- **Liquidity**: RealtyMogul REITs have quarterly redemption periods, giving slightly more liquidity than traditional private real estate investments. However, private placements and individual deals are generally illiquid, with holding periods of 3-10 years.

- **Fees**: For REITs, RealtyMogul charges a 1% asset management fee. For private placements, fees vary and may include acquisition, asset Each platform offers distinct benefits, so it's important to align your choice with your investment budget, liquidity needs, and experience level.

Side Hustle # 26 : Peer-to-Peer Lending: Invest in Loans for Passive Returns

If you have extra money sitting around in a savings account with a low-interest rate and would like it to generate a decent ROI without much time or effort needed from your end, then this is a hustle that you would want to consider. This is an investment model where you fund personal or business loans through online platforms like LendingClub, Prosper, or Upstart. Instead of a bank or other traditional institution providing the loan, investors like you contribute the capital. As the borrower repays the loan, you earn passive income through interest. This side hustle offers an appealing balance of flexibility, passive income, and moderate capital requirements, making it a viable option if you're seeking returns over time without constant hands-on effort.

Time Commitment and Earnings Potential:

In terms of time commitment, P2P lending is largely hands-off. After setting up your account and deciding on your investment strategy, you can automate loan funding and let the platform handle repayment tracking. Many P2P platforms also allow you to diversify across multiple loans, spreading out your investment to reduce risk.

On average, you can expect annual returns in the range of 4-7%, though higher returns are possible with riskier loans. The amount you earn will vary based on the platform and the types of loans you choose, so expect returns to correlate directly with your risk tolerance.

Getting Started: Actionable Steps

1. **Research Platforms**: Start by exploring different P2P lending platforms to see which best aligns with your financial goals, available investment amount, and risk tolerance. LendingClub, Prosper, and Upstart are popular choices, each with its own strengths. For example, LendingClub offers a mix of personal and small business loans, while Prosper has a strong focus on personal loans.

2. **Set an Investment Budget**: Determine how much capital you're willing to invest. Most platforms have a low minimum (often around $25-100 per loan), allowing you to invest incrementally and diversify across multiple loans.

3. **Choose Loan Risk Levels**: Decide on the types of loans you're comfortable with—higher-risk loans generally offer higher returns but come with increased chances of default. Many platforms categorize loans by risk level, making it easier to choose based on your comfort level.

4. **Automate Investments**: Most P2P platforms offer automated investing, allowing you to set criteria for loans you want to fund (such as credit score, loan purpose, or risk level) and automatically allocate funds.

5. **Monitor Returns and Adjust**: Track your returns over time and periodically adjust your strategy if needed. Some investors choose to reinvest their earnings to compound returns, while others withdraw them as a source of steady income.

P2P lending can be an effective passive income stream if you're looking for a relatively low-maintenance, low to medium-risk investment. As with any investment, understanding the platform's loan grading system and thoroughly researching each platform's fees and terms will help ensure you make the most of your P2P lending experience.

If you believe this is a good fit for you, then you can give this gig a shot...

Side Hustle # 27 : Dividend Stock Investing: Earning Passive Income through Dividends

Dividend stock investing is a long-term investment strategy where you buy shares in companies that pay regular dividends. These dividends are typically paid quarterly and can offer a steady, passive income stream. By building a portfolio of dividend-paying stocks, you earn money as companies distribute a portion of their profits to shareholders. This side hustle is attractive for those looking for a gradual way to build wealth and enjoy periodic income, with the potential to reinvest dividends to compound growth over time.

Time Commitment and Earnings Potential:

The time commitment for dividend stock investing is relatively low once you have chosen your stocks and established your portfolio. You'll likely spend some initial time researching, selecting stocks, and setting up your brokerage account, but after that, it's generally a passive strategy. Many investors review their portfolio periodically (monthly, quarterly, or annually) to check on performance and adjust holdings if needed.

Average returns vary widely based on market conditions and the specific stocks chosen, but dividend yields often range from 2-5% annually, with additional gains possible if stock prices increase. For example, a $5,000 investment with a 4% dividend yield would yield about $200 per year in dividends alone.

Getting Started: Actionable Steps:

1. **Set Up a Brokerage Account**: Start by setting up an investment account with a brokerage that supports dividend stock investing. Platforms like Vanguard, Fidelity, and Robinhood are popular and offer beginner-friendly options. Look for brokers with low fees to maximize your returns.

2. **Determine Your Investment Budget**: Decide how much you're willing to invest upfront and whether you plan to contribute monthly. Dividend investing works well even with small, consistent contributions, so you don't need a huge capital base to get started.

3. **Research Dividend Stocks**: Look for companies with a strong track record of consistent dividend payments. Many investors target Dividend Aristocrats—companies that have increased their dividends annually for at least 25 years—for reliable, long-term growth.

4. **Consider Dividend Reinvestment**: Many brokerages offer Dividend Reinvestment Plans (DRIPs), which automatically reinvest your dividends back into the same stock. This compounding effect can significantly boost returns over time.

5. **Monitor and Rebalance Your Portfolio**: Periodically review your portfolio to see how each stock is performing. You may want to diversify your holdings across sectors (such as tech, healthcare, and utilities) to reduce risk.

Dividend stock investing is a relatively low-maintenance side hustle that can offer dependable passive income. By focusing on established companies with solid dividend histories, you'll be better positioned for steady returns that could complement or even replace part of your primary income over time.

If you believe this is a good fit for you, then you can give this gig a shot...

Side Hustle # 28 : Owning a vending machine

Owning and operating vending machines is an attractive side hustle for many because it can offer passive income with minimal time investment once set up. The vending machine industry is vast, covering snacks, beverages, healthy options, and even specialty items like electronics or beauty products. Typically, vending machine owners earn between $50 to $200 per month per machine, depending on the machine's location and the type of products sold. High-traffic areas, such as office buildings, schools, or gyms, can yield higher returns, potentially pushing monthly earnings to $500 or more. Initial costs for purchasing and stocking a machine can range from $1,000 to $5,000, but this investment can pay off quickly with the right placement and product mix.

Time Commitment and Average Earning Potential:

After the initial setup, vending machines require occasional restocking, cleaning, and maintenance, which can typically be done in a few hours per week. If you own multiple machines, expect to dedicate more time, especially in high-traffic areas where products sell quickly. However, once you're familiar with the routine, managing a few machines can be done in a day or two each month.

The average earnings potential for a vending machine business varies widely, depending on factors like the number of machines owned, product selection, machine location, and customer traffic. Generally:

- **Single Vending Machine:** One vending machine in a high-traffic area (like a break room, school, or gym) can earn between $50 to $200 per month, depending on product pricing and demand.
- **Multiple Machines:** With around 10 well-placed machines, earnings can reach $500 to $2,000 monthly. Experienced operators often report that 20 or more machines can bring in around $4,000 to $10,000 monthly in gross revenue.

Here are the steps to help you get started:

1. **Research & Decide on Product Focus**: Determine what type of products you want to sell. Common choices include snacks, beverages, or healthy options. Consider the needs of your target area, like offices or schools, which can inform what to stock.
2. **Choose a Vending Machine Type**: There are new, used, and refurbished vending machines available. While used machines cost less, new machines often come with warranties, reducing maintenance worries. Look for models that accept both cash and card payments to appeal to more customers.
3. **Secure a Location**: Finding a profitable location is essential. Contact local businesses, gyms, schools, or office buildings to ask about placing a machine in their space. Some places may charge a

small commission, but high-traffic locations can yield much higher returns.

4. **Stock & Monitor**: Begin by purchasing a small initial inventory to test which items sell best. Use tracking sheets or apps to monitor stock levels, sales, and expiration dates. Restock and adjust your offerings based on which items perform well.

5. **Manage Maintenance & Customer Needs**: Ensure you're prepared for minor repairs or can call a service provider. Respond to customer feedback if certain products are requested, and keep machines clean and functional to build customer trust.

Owning a vending machine can be a rewarding side hustle, offering scalable and flexible income with just a small commitment of time once you're up and running.

Here's a list of reputable places where you can buy vending machines, including options for new, used, or refurbished machines:

1. **Vending.com** : Known for a wide selection of new machines, including snacks, drinks, and combination machines, with financing options available.

2. **eBay** : A large marketplace with many sellers offering both new and used vending machines. Great for finding budget options, but always check seller ratings and reviews.

3. **Craigslist** : Local listings may offer vending machines at lower prices. This can be useful for finding affordable, used machines, but inspect before purchasing to ensure functionality.

4. **Facebook Marketplace** : Another local option with a wide range of used vending machines. Buyers can often negotiate prices, but it's important to meet sellers in person and assess machine condition.

5. **Global Vending Group** : Offers a wide variety of new, used, and refurbished vending machines, along with warranties and shipping options. They also provide support for beginners.
6. **Amazon** : Sells both new and refurbished vending machines, primarily smaller and countertop models. Reviews from previous buyers can be helpful for quality assurance.
7. **A&M Equipment Sales** : Specializes in refurbished machines and also provides maintenance parts and tech support. Ideal if you want a machine that looks and works like new at a lower price.
8. **Vending World** : Based in California, Vending World offers used and refurbished machines, specializing in soda and snack models. They provide warranties on refurbished machines and ship nationwide.
9. **UsedVending.com** : A large online marketplace where sellers list both food trucks and vending machines. They have a variety of options for snack, drink, combo, and specialty machines, with customer service support available.
10. **VEII (Vending Equipment Inc.)** : Known for quality refurbished machines, with a warranty and support for repairs. They also offer technical training on vending machine maintenance if you're new to the business.

Here's a list of popular software and apps that vending machine owners can use to monitor inventory levels, track sales, and manage operations:

1. **VendSoft** : Designed for vending machine management, VendSoft tracks inventory, monitors stock levels, and generates detailed sales reports. It also allows route optimization for efficient refilling and reduces out-of-stock issues.
2. **Parlevel Systems** : A comprehensive solution for vending operators, Parlevel's management software integrates telemetry to

provide real-time inventory updates, sales reports, and machine status monitoring. It's ideal for managing large numbers of machines.

3. **Cantaloupe (formerly USA Technologies ePort)** : This app-based platform provides cashless payment processing, telemetry, and sales tracking. The system offers insights into stock levels and performance metrics, allowing owners to optimize operations and plan restocking trips.

4. **MoMa Vending** : The MoMa (Mobile Management) app offers real-time sales and inventory monitoring. It provides low-stock alerts and item-level reporting, helping owners streamline restocking schedules and track popular items.

5. **Vend-Trak** : Vend-Trak is a cloud-based inventory tracking software for vending machines, allowing for remote monitoring of stock, sales reports, and machine performance. The platform is accessible on mobile and desktop, ideal for flexible use.

6. **Seaga Smartware** : This app works with Seaga vending machines and provides insights into stock levels, sales data, and machine alerts. It's helpful for those using Seaga machines to track item popularity and reduce stockouts.

7. **Smart Vending Solutions** : This software is geared toward vending businesses looking for real-time data on machine stock levels, product sales, and cash collections. It also has reporting tools to help track overall performance.

8. **VendSoft Mobile App** : VendSoft's mobile app pairs with their desktop software, allowing on-the-go monitoring of inventory levels, sales, and route tracking. The app is ideal for operators who manage multiple machines and need to stay updated remotely.

9. **eVending** : eVending software integrates with compatible vending machines to provide live inventory tracking, cashless payment options, and performance analytics. It's best for those who want

remote control over their vending machine operations.

10. **VMS (Vending Management Software) by Nayax :** Known for cashless payment systems, Nayax's VMS offers telemetry features that provide inventory management, sales tracking, and machine health monitoring. It's an all-in-one solution for vending operators looking to scale.

Side Hustle # 29 : Owning an ATM Machine

This one is similar to the vending machine gig for the most part except for what's being dispensed from the machine. Both have unique advantages and disadvantages, but you can decide for yourself on which one makes the most sense to you. Owning an ATM machine can allow you to earn passive income by providing convenient cash access to customers. This business model involves purchasing or leasing an ATM and placing it in a high-traffic location such as a convenience store, bar, or gas station. You earn money through transaction fees charged to users each time they withdraw cash. With a well-placed machine, you can generate a steady stream of income without requiring extensive hands-on management.

Time Commitment and Earning Potential:

The time commitment for owning an ATM machine is relatively low compared to other side hustles. After the initial setup, your primary responsibilities include maintaining the machine, replenishing cash, and monitoring transaction activity, which can typically be managed in just a few hours per week.

The average earning potential varies based on location, transaction volume, and fees charged but can range from $300 to $2,000 per month per machine. High-traffic areas with limited ATM access can lead to even higher earnings, especially if you charge competitive transaction fees.

To start your ATM business, follow these actionable steps:

1. **Research and Understand the Market**: Familiarize yourself with local regulations regarding ATM placement and transaction fees. Identify high-traffic locations in your area that lack nearby ATMs.
2. **Choose Your Business Model**: Decide whether you want to purchase your ATM outright or lease it. Owning your machine provides greater profit margins but requires a higher upfront investment. Refer to the detailed section below that explains the pros and cons for each model to help you make a better decision.
3. **Secure Funding**: Determine your budget for purchasing or leasing an ATM, including costs for installation, cash loading, maintenance, and insurance. You may need to apply for a small business loan or use personal savings.
4. **Purchase or Lease an ATM**: Research reputable ATM suppliers or manufacturers to purchase or lease your machine. Look for options that offer technical support and warranty coverage.
5. **Select a Location**: Approach business owners in high-traffic areas about placing your ATM on their premises. Negotiate an agreement that outlines the terms, including profit-sharing and maintenance responsibilities.
6. **Install and Set Up the ATM**: Work with your supplier to install

the ATM and ensure it's properly connected to the network for processing transactions. You'll need to set up the machine's software, including transaction fees.

7. **Replenish Cash Regularly**: Depending on transaction volume, ensure that you regularly refill the ATM with cash to avoid running out. This may involve coordinating with a cash-in-transit service or managing it yourself.

8. **Monitor Performance**: Use ATM management software to track transaction volume, fees collected, and maintenance needs. This will help you optimize operations and make informed decisions about future locations.

Let's try to understand the two types of ATM machine models and understand the nuances around each to help you make an informed decision on which would be the right option for you, in case you decided to proceed ahead with this side hustle.

Owning an ATM Machine

Investment:

- **Upfront Cost**: Buying an ATM machine outright generally requires a higher initial investment, which can range from $2,000 to $8,000 or more, depending on the machine's features and capabilities.
- **Ongoing Costs**: As an owner, you'll also be responsible for ongoing costs such as cash replenishment, maintenance, insurance, and any necessary software updates. Additionally, you may incur transaction processing fees paid to the network provider.

Benefits:

- **Higher Profit Margins**: Since you own the machine, you keep 100% of the transaction fees charged to users. This can lead to significantly higher profit margins, especially in high-traffic locations.
- **Asset Ownership**: An owned ATM is a tangible asset, and its value can appreciate over time. It can also be resold if you decide to exit the business.

Drawbacks:

- **Greater Financial Risk:** The upfront investment and ongoing maintenance costs present a financial risk, especially if the machine does not generate enough transactions to cover these expenses.
- **Time Commitment:** As an owner, you're responsible for managing the machine, including cash loading and maintenance, which requires a time commitment.

Leasing an ATM Machine

Investment:

- **Lower Upfront Cost:** Leasing an ATM usually involves a smaller initial investment, often requiring a down payment that may be significantly less than purchasing the machine outright. Monthly lease payments typically range from $50 to $200.
- **Additional Fees:** While leasing reduces the upfront financial burden, you may face additional fees, such as lease maintenance or transaction processing fees, which could affect overall profitability.

Benefits:

- **Reduced Risk:** Leasing lowers the initial financial risk, making it more accessible for beginners or those who want to test the ATM business model without a substantial investment.
- **Maintenance Support:** Many leasing agreements include maintenance support, meaning that if the machine requires repairs, the leasing company typically covers those costs, saving you time and money.

Drawbacks:

- **Lower Profit Margins:** With leasing, you may have to share a portion of the transaction fees with the leasing company, resulting in lower overall profits compared to owning.
- **No Asset Ownership:** Since you do not own the machine, you won't have the option to sell it for a profit later. Your financial return is primarily limited to the transaction fees generated while leasing.

In summary, owning an ATM machine typically involves a higher upfront investment but allows for greater profit potential and asset ownership. In contrast, leasing an ATM requires a lower initial investment and mitigates some financial risks but often results in lower profit margins and no asset ownership. Your decision should be guided by your financial capacity, risk tolerance, and long-term business goals.

Here's a list of places where you can buy or lease an ATM machine:

ATM Manufacturers

- **Nautilus Hyosung:** A leading manufacturer of ATMs, offering a variety of models suitable for different business needs. They provide options for purchasing and leasing.
- **Diebold Nixdorf:** Known for their advanced ATM technology and support services, they offer both leasing and purchase options.
- **Genmega:** Offers a range of ATMs with customizable options, including leasing and purchase plans.

ATM Distributors and Resellers

- **ATM Depot**: A reputable distributor of new and refurbished ATMs, providing options to buy or lease machines. They also offer financing solutions.
- **ATM Marketplace**: A comprehensive online resource that connects buyers with ATM sellers. You can find various options for purchasing and leasing machines from different vendors.
- **ATMs2Go**: Provides a variety of ATMs for sale or lease, along with maintenance and service packages.

Online Marketplaces

- **eBay**: A platform where individuals and businesses can buy and sell new or used ATMs. Make sure to verify the seller's reputation and warranty terms.
- **Craigslist**: Local classifieds where you may find used ATMs for sale. Exercise caution and conduct thorough research on sellers to avoid scams.

Financing and Leasing Companies

- **Banc of America Leasing & Capital**: Offers leasing solutions specifically for ATMs, along with financing options to buy new or used machines.
- **EverBank**: Provides equipment leasing solutions that include ATMs. They work with various manufacturers and offer customized financing packages.

ATM Franchise Opportunities

- **Cardtronics**: As a large ATM operator, they also offer franchise opportunities, allowing you to lease ATMs and have a ready-made support system.

- **National Cash Systems**: Provides ATM leasing services and offers a franchise opportunity to operate ATMs.

Local Banks and Credit Unions

- Many banks and credit unions may offer ATM leasing options for businesses. It's worth checking with your local financial institution to see if they have programs available.

Here's a list of software and apps that you can utilize to monitor the stock for ATM machines:

ATM Management Software

- **CPI ATM Management Software**: This software provides real-time monitoring of cash levels, transaction history, and alerts for low cash levels. It helps streamline cash management for ATM operators.
- **Nautilus Hyosung's NFS ATM Software**: Offers detailed reports on cash levels, transaction data, and performance metrics for Hyosung ATMs. This can be integrated into their ATM management solutions.

Inventory Management Software

- **Zoho Inventory**: This cloud-based software can help manage inventory levels for cash in ATMs, track stock, and automate reorder processes.
- **Sortly**: An easy-to-use inventory management app that can help users track the stock in their ATM machines, manage cash levels,

and monitor item movement.

Cash Management Solutions

- **Brink's Cash Management Solutions**: Provides a comprehensive cash management platform that helps monitor cash levels across multiple ATMs, allowing for better forecasting and inventory control.
- **CashTech**: This software helps ATM operators manage cash flow, monitor stock levels, and optimize cash replenishment schedules.

Mobile Apps for ATM Monitoring

- **ATM Manager**: A mobile app that allows operators to track ATM performance, cash levels, and transactions in real time. It can send notifications for low cash or other operational alerts.
- **ATM Tracker**: This app provides users with insights into cash levels and transaction history, helping to manage the stock effectively.

Reporting Tools

- **Microsoft Excel or Google Sheets**: While not specific to ATM monitoring, these tools can be customized to track cash levels and transactions. Operators can create dashboards to visualize stock levels and performance metrics.
- **Tableau**: A powerful data visualization tool that can be used to create custom reports on ATM performance, cash levels, and other metrics based on the data collected from ATMs.

Third-Party Monitoring Services

- **AccessCash**: This service provides remote monitoring and management of ATMs, including cash level tracking, transaction reporting, and alerts for maintenance needs.
- **ATMeye**: A cloud-based monitoring service that provides detailed reporting on cash levels, transaction volumes, and potential issues with ATMs.

Here are some things you should consider before choosing a software:

- **Integration**: Ensure that the software can integrate with your existing ATM systems for seamless monitoring.
- **User-Friendly**: Look for intuitive interfaces that make it easy to track stock levels and performance metrics.
- **Scalability**: Choose software that can grow with your business, especially if you plan to expand your ATM network.

Support and Updates: Opt for software providers that offer reliable customer support and regular updates to ensure your systems are running smoothly.

5

Conclusion

Congratulations on reaching the end of this guide to side hustles! You've taken significant steps towards expanding your income opportunities and gaining financial independence. Throughout this book, we've explored a variety of side hustles, from those requiring little to no investment to those leveraging specialized skills or capital. Whether you're flipping thrift store finds, designing print-on-demand products, or investing in dividend stocks, each option offers unique advantages that can align with your interests, skills, and resources. While this guide was meant to help you generate some ideas on potential opportunities that you can consider

As you embark on your side hustle journey, remember that the most important part is to take action. Start small, stay consistent, and remain open to learning as you navigate your new ventures. Many successful entrepreneurs began with just a simple idea or passion, so don't underestimate the potential of your own skills and interests. Keep track of your progress, celebrate your achievements, and be prepared to adapt along the way.

Your journey doesn't end here; it's just the beginning. I encourage you to share your experiences, learn from others, and continue exploring new opportunities as you work toward financial freedom. If you found this book helpful, please consider leaving a review on Amazon. Your feedback not only helps me improve future editions but also assists fellow readers in finding valuable resources for their own side hustle adventures. With that I will leave you with this quote to give you something to ponder about.

"Thinking will not overcome fear, but action will."
– W. Clement Stone

Hence, take the next step and act towards the goals and dreams you have set for yourself. Believe in yourself and take that leap of faith and dive deep into the next phase of your life and shape your life into exactly what you dreamt of. You have full control of your destiny! Remember, that all accomplishments in life begin with a dream. A dream then turns into ambition and helps pave the way for goals. A goal helps you define the timeline for when you want to achieve it by and what actions you need to take to get there. Actions demand a plan or an outline of steps that can help you get started. All of that begins with one single thought or an idea. And that's exactly what this book and/or guide was meant to do for you, is to help you come up with that one or more idea(s) that you best fit your situation to help you get started. You've already taken the first step towards your goals and dreams by getting this book and you've shown commitment and dedication by finishing it. So congratulations on winning the hardest battle which is to start and act. From here on out, it just gets better.

With that I Thank you for reading, and sincerely wish you success in all your future endeavors! Enjoy the journey and the process.

With that, Go give **YOURSELF** a shot…at your dreams!

THE END.

6

Resources

A CE- https://www.acefitness.org/fitness-certifications/personal-trainer-certification/default.aspx

NASM- https://www.nasm.org/become-a-personal-trainer?cq_cmp=1720933128&network=g&utm_term=national%20academy%20of%20sports%20medicine&utm_campaign=cpt-pros-traffic-search-branded&utm_source=google&utm_medium=ppc&hsa_acc=2454829191&hsa_cam=1720933128&hsa_grp=98336128005&hsa_ad=715536242819&hsa_src=g&hsa_tgt=kwd-772024464&hsa_kw=national%20academy%20of%20sports%20medicine&hsa_mt=e&hsa_net=adwords&hsa_ver=3&gad_source=1&gclid=Cj0KCQjw7Py4BhCbARIsAMMx-_LF9rXSs93BZwMDG0GUMANV38T_Fy74_uOftpFGYKNMruVWKyX3PGMaAkY1EALw_wcB

ISSA- https://www.issaonline.com/certification/how-to-become-a-personal-trainer?cq_src=google_ads&cq_cmp=21363476878&cq_con=166237062427&cq_term=issa%20personal%20trainer%20certification&cq_med=&cq_plac=&cq_net=g&cq_pos=&cq_plt=gp&utm_medium=Paid_Search&utm_source=Google&utm_campaign=US_S

earch_Conv_Lead_Brand_Priority_Max_Conversions&utm_conten
t=CPT&utm_term=issa%20personal%20trainer%20certification&ke
yword=issa%20personal%20trainer%20certification&cq_cmp=21363
476878&cq_plac=&cq_net=g&cq_pos=&gad_source=1&gclid=Cj0K
CQjw7Py4BhCbARIsAMMx-_KfWzyVKuqP3SlhbhNTjja9qE_evm8
OQJrTW7EP-iJ1bFEZdPJj31AaArqBEALw_wcB

ACSM- https://www.acsm.org/certification?gad_source=1&gclid=C
j0KCQjw7Py4BhCbARIsAMMx-_K94N-9y4jEYtDE7eMUdQctcRn
NNjFaVZPJRkspPKYOvYX6H2l12W4aAutzEALw_wcB

NSCA - https://www.nsca.com/certification/nsca-cpt/?srsltid=AfmB
OopQru918dq4vHSB6XElLiMm0p5rKWVTXRp76WT74NsXFsam
7fKb

OpenAI. (2024). *ChatGPT* (Version 4.0) [AI language model]. Retrieved
from https://www.openai.com/chatgpt